WHEN SIN
WAS SYONAN-TO

Bright Singapore
2000.

WHEN SINGAPORE WAS SYONAN-TO

N.I. LOW

TIMES BOOKS INTERNATIONAL
Singapore • Kuala Lumpur

© 1973 Low Ngiong Ing

This edition published in 1995 by
Times Books International
an imprint of Times Editions Pte Ltd
Times Centre
1 New Industrial Road
Singapore 1953

Times Subang
Lot 46, Subang Hi-Tech Industrial Park
Batu Tiga
40000 Shah Alam
Selangor Darul Ehsan
Malaysia

Printed in Singapore

ISBN 981 204 614 3

Contents

About the Author

N.I. Low was born in a village in Foochow in 1900. His tailor father, on going bankrupt, migrated to Singapore with his family. He was orphaned at the age of nine years, his parents dying of cholera within six days of each other, and he worked as a house servant for food and lodging. An Englishman paid for his schooling. He was awarded a Straits Settlements Government Scholarship in 1919. In 1923, he began his career as a teacher and subsequently became principal, Supervisor of Private Schools, Education Officer, and lecturer at the Teachers' Training College.

His book is largely based on *This Singapore*, a book privately printed and distributed in 1947. A great deal of the material was contributed by the late Cheng Hui Ming, who was Assistant to the Secretary for Chinese Affairs in Singapore and consequently had access to information not available to the general public.

1   Singapore, Impregnable Fortress

It was early February 1942.

We were doomed. But we indignantly put the thought away from us. Singapore was a shambles. But we assured ourselves that all would end well. The day of miracles was not over, surely.

Jap bombers zoomed low. We could almost make out the faces of the pilots. They raked us with machine-guns. The sirens no longer whined. It was a never-ending alert.

A million or more were trapped in this doomed city, this Bastion of Empire, this Isle Inviolate, this Impregnable Fortress. But among us, the doomed, was a calm, an assurance that is difficult to understand in the retrospect. Were we too dazed to realise the precariousness of our position? Were our hearts too much engaged to allow us to accept the truth?

We did not realise that one miracle at least was happening in our midst — the miracle of our own gullibility to propaganda. And to rumours. It was a great day for the rumour-monger. No rumour, however fantastic, fell on rocky soil, but sprouted and flourished exceedingly in our fevered imaginations. Twenty thousand Chinese soldiers had arrived. Men had seen them marching from the wharves. The Americans had landed at Mersing. Men had heard the news over the wireless.

Every concrete building was crammed with refugees. The ground floor of the Cathay Building alone had thousands. Among us were many soldiers. They had thrown away their arms. We showed no resentment. Far from looking askance at them, we shared what we had with them. We glozed over the uncomplimentary implications of their presence. They were no heroes. Neither were we. They had done their poor best. That was enough for us. We accepted them as companions in misfortune.

The agony was intensified on Sunday, 15th February. But suddenly, at about 5 o'clock in the afternoon, a long wail from a siren sounded and pandemonium abruptly ended. The ensuing silence was uncanny. But for many it did not mean rest from their labours. Certainly not for the M.A.S. people. They had to go on spending themselves.

Soldiers with sunken eyes and battle-worn clothes straggled in. They had fought unavailingly for the past thirty-six hours. Said one Tommy, as he was having a much-needed wash and drink in a Chinese house, "Well, it's over. I hope I'll be sent home soon. We'll settle accounts later." Poor boy, little did he know what was in store for him. And for that matter, little did we ourselves know what was in store for us.

But we did know enough to realise that some of us, tired as we were, should know no rest until one task was done. Those who had books, especially Chinese books, went through them to destroy everything compromising. A few dug holes in their gardens and buried the lot. It was a wise measure, born of the experience of our brethren in China, who had preceded us on the road to our Calvary.

The women got to work to sew Japanese flags for the morrow's use. Enterprising householders stole marches on their neighbours by getting ready posters bearing messages of welcome, hoping thereby to ingratiate themselves with their incoming masters.

These precautions taken, we slept. Next morning, plasters of a fiery red (the Rising Sun of Japan) sprouted on all front doors. None was so foolhardy as to indulge any itch for singularity. Representatives of all the communities

2

except the Chinese went to Bukit Timah to welcome the conquerors. The Chinese were not represented, as their leaders had made themselves scarce. They were all tarred with anti-Japanism, having had some connection or other with the 'China Relief Fund' — an euphemism for contributions made to China's war-chest. As the Japanese swung by in formation, some clapped hands, some fluttered flags, and a few Chinese who were present looked sheepish, glowered on by the conquerors.

They got the lion's share of the bear-baiting of the civilians that soon followed. One Chinaman had a grandstand view of the proceedings, safely but inconspicuously ensconced on the first floor of a shop in Rumah Miskin. They slapped and slapped, and never got tired of slapping, and nearly all the faces slapped happened to be Chinese faces. One marvelled at the assiduity and enthusiasm with which the Japanese slapped. One marvelled too at the thickness of their palms. For a change, they would kick a Chinaman down, bid him pick himself up and then kneel down, pommel him with their fists or belabour him with the stocks of their rifles or put stones on his head, and these he had to keep on. A second variation of the theme was to induce two Chinamen, by gentle persuasions, to slap each other.

Japanese soldiers went round requisitioning cars. Car owners surrendered ignition keys with as good a grace as they could muster.

Civilian homes had visits from Japanese soldiers. Some of these were domiciliary; most of them unauthorised and casual — to satisfy curiosity or to forage for supplies and amenities. Mosquito nets and mattresses were informally requisitioned, the soldiers helping themselves to any that suited them. Next they rummaged for clothes. They confined themselves, however, to serviceable things like plain white shirts and khaki trousers, spurning luxurious things. Possessors of sewing-machines had soldier visitors, many of whom rewarded the seamstresses handsomely with goods which were not their own.

3

After campaigning in the jungle for weeks, such conduct was understandable. They found themselves in a land of sartorial plenty and sensibly relieved the helots of a little of their superfluity.

But it did not end there. From helping themselves to what could fairly be regarded as necessaries, they went on to laying hands on whatever took their fancy. Watches had an irresistible attraction for all, and jewellery for some. They relieved the original owners of trinkets that they were so callously flaunting even at that calamitous time.

The joy of possession soon palled on some of these recent arrivals in Eldorado. Things taken from one house were sometimes shed in the very next. One young soldier annexed a shaving-set and left a pair of spectacles in exchange. Another had a cup of coffee in a rich man's house and gave thanks for his entertainment by giving his host a diamond ring.

The raping varied in intensity. Some localities suffered more and some less. As was natural, it varied also according to the characters of individual soldiers. Their victims steeled themselves to accept the inevitable. But not even charity, Christian or heathen, could make a man forgive easily a fellow-townsman, though of another race and creed, playing the bear-leader to Japanese, pointing out this house and that and saying *"Sini ada perempuan cantik"* — there is a beautiful girl here. The Upper Serangoon area was among the most fortunate. The commanding officer must have been more squeamish or more of a martinet. The he-men under his command had to rein themselves in by day, prowling about and chalking up mentally the lairs of their quarries, and going in for the kill under cover of darkness.

Barricades had gone up all over Singapore, at which all were searched before they were allowed to proceed, or were refused passage, as the whims of the sentry dictated. At one barricade a Chinese pedalling a loaded tricycle was told to stop. He did so, but the moment the sentry turned away to deal with someone else, he made off as fast as he could. He was overtaken and manhandled, made to kneel down and was clouted on the head until he fainted. When he came to, he was thrashed until he fainted again. All this was done in the sight of hundreds of pedestrians who passed that way, and had a salutary effect on them. Thenceforward the sentry did not find his duties too onerous. Every order was instantly obeyed, and if he playfully dropped his rifle on a foot, the victim smiled appreciation for the signal favour.

That sentry was neither more zealous nor more brutal than his fellows. He was, as would seem, of a more kindly disposition than most, for when someone presented a slip of paper bearing the inscription in Japanese — "Please let me pass; I'm looking for my family," — he let the man pass at once. But he could ill-treat the tricyclist, and many others, whom after manhandling, he made to kneel by the roadside for hours, giving them his wrathful attention whenever he felt inclined! One must conclude that it was an instance of imperfect sympathy, neither understanding the other's point of view. How could the Japanese soldier, accustomed to giving instant and unquestioning obedience to orders, and on occasion to receiving them, how could he understand the slovenly Chinese who seemed so inclined to greet an order with airy badinage and to brush it aside with a wave of the hand? How could he, to whom chastisement was a matter of routine, which he received from a superior and administered to a subordinate, how could he understand the resentment that smouldered in the eyes of the Chinese whom he had so justly punished? No wonder he was exasperated, and dealt all the more savagely with the offenders.

The Chinaman, on his side, with his inherited and ingrained misprizing of all that appertained to war, was incapable of understanding the Japanese sentry. How could he know that the Japanese was such a fanatic for discipline, loving it for its own sake, as the only key to the enigma of life, that to him a command was sacrosanct, tardy compliance with which was not a mere peccadillo, as the Chinese fondly imagined, but an affront to the Emperor himself? As for failure to bow to him, the sentry, it was sacrilege, for he, the sentry, was the vicegerent for the nonce of *Tenno Heika* — that very god of very god, child of the Moon Goddess, holding sway over gods and men.

2   Our Nip Masters at Closer Range

In the days that followed we saw our new masters at closer range.

They had a liking for bicycles, we saw. Passing cyclists were halted, and if their mounts were at all presentable, they were incontinently relieved of them. Those hardened sinners, "unfruitful of good and unprofitable in all ways", the unmentionable Chinese, of course, had no right to any consideration and were sent packing with a slap or two to salve their loss. But our Nip masters did not treat the other communities, Indians and Malays, in so cavalier a fashion. They had a more tender regard for their own reputation. Thieving was unknown in Japan; in Tokyo no doors were ever locked. A soldier of the Imperial Army never helped himself to anything that he did not pay for. He paid in full measure and over. So all non-Chinese losers of bicycles received a dollar, or even more. One Indian who surrendered a new 'Raleigh' actually got four dollars.

A second instance of our new masters' regard for personal and national honour came from Malacca. A company was quartered for a night at one of the wards of the General Hospital there. Next morning, after the night's lodgers had departed, the Matron went over the linen and in dismay, more to herself than to the assisting nurse, remarked on the many losses of bed-sheets and pillow-cases. Within an hour the company was back at the hospital. The Matron was summoned. The company was paraded in her honour. The company commander informed her that she had insulted the Imperial Forces by her suspicions, and deserved punishment. Would she apologise and confess that she had made an error in counting? She apologised, and the company marched away, honour satisfied.

A host of Japanophils had for forty years and more told us that the Japanese were the Greeks of our time, lovers of plain living and high thinking. An incident outside the Municipal Building, Singapore, bore out the claim so frequently made for them that they were lovers of plain living. A Chinaman, spruce and dapper, was passing in a rickshaw. A Japanese soldier stopped the rickshaw, pulled the Chinaman down and, firmly grasping him by his tie, gave him a good shaking. Next he motioned the puller to climb on to the seat and made the dandy pull the rickshaw in his turn. This Robin Hood-like behaviour of the Japanese soldier was rather taking.

Equally taking was the unashamed way of the average Japanese soldier of discharging the minor obligations of nature with' an easy grace — at the roadside. He had none of our prudishness. Like the Greek of classical times, he was not ashamed of his body and his concerns.

Think, too, of that Japanese officer who boarded the automatic lift at the Supreme Court and did not issue from it until he had gone up and down nine times. When he did issue from it, his face was wreathed in smiles.

Even the sartorial vanity of the Japanese officer was amusing. There were hordes of them gadding about the town, their swords too long for many of them, in their tweed uniforms. Tweed was unsuitable for this hot and damp climate. But tweed was apparently the correct material for officers of the *Mikado's* army, and they sought to mitigate the consequent odoriferousness in a generous use of powerful scents. A touch of vanity made the whole world kin. A vain man we could understand and even like.

But had our new masters nothing more to show us?

7

They were wrong in thinking that we were ill-disposed and difficult to please. It is human nature to worship the rising star and strive to hitch one's wagon to that star.

Said a Eurasian woman at the time, "Haven't the British played us a dirty trick!" Her hearer could not but agree. The sense of being the victims of a base desertion rankled in the minds of all of us. The memory of that unseemly stampeding from Penang still had its sting, of launches cleared of Asiatic women at the point of the bayonet, and of our chagrin and disgust when, going to the railway-station to meet relatives and friends, we saw no Asiatics in that wilderness of Europeans, whom the Governor was receiving as if they were conquering heroes come. No, the Japanese were mistaken. We were not ill-disposed towards them. On the contrary, we were anxious to see whatever good there was in them. With what alacrity and what inward satisfaction we passed on the story of the Japanese officer who had dealt out summary punishment on his men for assaulting civilians! We realised that the Japanese were our conquerors. Let them win our homage as well, compelling us to assent to the workings of fate by showing signs of a high nobility.

Was not courage enough? No, it was not. For we had seen courage among ourselves. The 'Dalforce', made up of young Chinese Communists and jail-birds who had gone out to meet the incoming Japanese after only a week's training and armed with obsolete rifles, who by their desperate valour had stemmed the Japanese advance in their sector for half a day and who, dying, had left the rest of us, their compatriots, to pay the piper for their swan-song of heroism — these had shown courage, surely. That girl in her teens marching between Japanese soldiers to death or a worse fate, who, coming to a barricade where a Eurasian was in difficulties with the sentry, could be so unmindful of her own troubles as to stop and interpret for that man and extricate him — surely this girl showed courage. Surely Lady Thomas showed courage when she elected to stay and share the tribulations that were coming to the women of this land. The nurse in Malacca who, bidding farewell to her charges in the Maternity Ward and hearing their cries and implorings, could so master her own fears as to volunteer to stay, letting her companions go to Singapore and safety — surely that nurse showed courage. And the men and women and children for whom Providence and the British Government had made fewest provisions, whose only acquaintance with the British Empire took the form of harassings by the police inspectors and their myrmidons, what did they do when they saw the British and Australian P.O.W.'s in the streets, cleaning up and scavengering and looking so famished and so disconsolate? Did they slink away, stifling pangs of pity? If they did slink away, it was to prepare presents of food and cigarettes for the P.O.W.'s. Receiving gifts from them, did the P.O.W.'s still think of them as dirty Chinks and scum of the earth, or as very gallant men and women and children? Some were tied to lamp posts and given a pasting, when caught. And yet there were some who went on indulging their foolish compassion, in spite of the tale that flew from mouth to mouth to the effect that one silly woman had been held up by her legs and her head dashed on the ground. Surely, these showed courage of no mean order.

We said to ourselves that our Nip masters had to show us more than courage to win our homage. In what other ways were they our superiors? Wisdom had to be justified in the Japs, her favourite children, and in us, her step-children.

Yes, they beat us by their lust. Individual soldiers roamed into our houses. They good-humouredly turned over photograph albums. Woe unto us if we had pictures of pretty girls! They would demand a peep at the originals, and as likely as not cut up rough if we failed to produce them.

They rounded up women from the countryside, pinning on to each a tab in Chinese 'For Military Use'. They rounded up all the sing-song girls, dance hostesses, prostitutes, their operations directed by our Formosan friends who had not lived among us for many years in vain.

They took into custody one of our foremost fellow-townsmen, one conversant with the haunts and habits of large numbers of these lights-o'-love. A wily Chink, he tried to keep a few cards up his sleeve so that he might meet the demands of the Japanese Military Police, their Army, their Navy and their Air Force. Surely all the various sections of the Japanese armed forces had equal claims on him. Who was he to show preference? Poor man, trying to please all, he ended by pleasing none, and had to run the gauntlet of successive displeasures.

At the concentration camps, some girls were so foolish as not to relish the prospect of receiving Jap attentions. Some cut their hair short, hoping to pass off as boys. These did not do justice to the keenness of scent and of eye of the Japanese. They were routed out and carted away.

How was this carrion disposed of? They were sent into 'comfort' homes — the more toothsome for the officers and the less for the lower ranks.

Part of Cairnhill Road was palisaded off to provide a Yoshiwara quarter for the Japanese rank and file. Some qualified male nurses, called 'dressers' in those days, were seconded from our hospitals for ablution duties. One of them was given quarters for his family inside the stockade. He became a fluent speaker of *Nippon-go,* which was what we called the Japanese language in those days, out of respect for our new masters. The Japanese were *Nippon-jin* and their language *Nippon-go.* We had to be careful. A slip of the tongue might earn us a slap.

On 6th March 1946, six months after the collapse of Japan, a party of fifteen girls landed in Singapore. They had served as comfort girls in Java for nearly four years. Said one to the man whose duty it was to receive them at the wharfside, "Will my father have me back?"

Had our Nip masters anything more to show us, something that might warm our veins with a draught or two of generosity and magnanimity? Something that might make us acquiesce to the dispensation of fate and say that they deserved to win? Had they anything comparable to the generosity that would one day prompt a British general to say that while all armies talk of fighting to the last man, it was only the Japanese Army that did; anything comparable to the magnanimity that would one day make Lord Louis Mountbatten issue a peremptory order that all bear-baiting of Nips must cease forthwith; anything comparable to the chivalry that would one day glow so movingly in the quiet tones of MacArthur's pronouncement on Yamashita? The Japanese did indeed throw a wreath into the sea, at the spot where the *Prince of Wales* and the *Repulse* had gone down, and they published letters from Sir Shenton-Thomas and Generals Wainwright and Percival thanking the Governor-General of Formosa for gifts of cigarettes. But somehow we felt a persisting ache of heart. These supposedly magnanimous gestures did not have the authentic note of magnanimity. They were theatrical and sounded hollow. They did not make our spirits less forlorn.

During those weary months the Japanese were condemned in the conscience of the common man of this land they had conquered. We were not unmindful of their claims of cousinhood, of community of blood and culture. They shamed us, fellow-Mongols and fellow-Asiatics, by their failure to display generosity and magnanimity and chivalry in the day of their triumph. Against our will we had to say of them what Montaigne said of the Germans many hundreds of years ago:

"Cursed be these men: for they know neither pity nor honour!"

Shortly after the Jap entry I saw something that impressed me — a Jap private taking his punishment at the hands of a staff officer. He stood ramrod straight while resounding blows rained upon him, with the palm and the back of the hand, and his eyes remained, unclouded. Was I witnessing an exhibition of the *Samurai* spirit? That picture of manly submission to lawful authority will remain with me as long as I live.

I was lying sick and alone in my house, like a stricken animal creeping into his lair to die unseen. One day, among the many Jap visitors I had, was a young man who came again the same night, alone, bringing me medicine. He did the same thing night after night. We could not communicate, he knowing neither English nor Chinese, and I knowing no Japanese. His medicine did me little good, but his kind intention did me much good. On the eve of his departure for Sumatra, he drove a couple of cars into my compound and gave me the ignition keys.

3   The Wrath of Yamashita

We were nobody's darlings, we Chinese. We weren't Yamashita's. The further south he got, the less he loved us. A man might suddenly catch sight of a black flag. Woe betide him if he was caught sight of, for that flag spelt death for all Chinese in its path.

The desperadoes of the Dalforce were the last straw for Yamashita. He made up his mind that the Chinese community should be cauterized. The instrument he selected was the Second Field *Kempeitai* (Japanese Military Police), which had been forged and tempered in Manchuria and could be counted on to perform the operation neatly, expeditiously and without too much fuss or sentiment. There was to be no loss of time, as the Sumatran campaign was impending.

No time was lost. The day after the Fall of Singapore, Lt. Col. Satoru Oishi, Officer Commanding the Second Field *Kempeitai,* called a meeting at Fort Canning, at which a plan was agreed on for the extirpation of all undesirable elements of the Chinese community.

On the afternoon of the 17th, Japanese Military Police went round among us, the Chinese, instructing us to concentrate at specified points. We were warned that we might be away for a few days and should provide ourselves with food and water.

Speculation was rife among the Chinese. What was the purpose of this merry wake? None could give an authoritative answer. We guessed and guessed. To listen to a lecture on our past misdemeanours, on our new status and our new duties, said some. To receive 'good citizen' badges, said others. To furnish volunteers for a ten-day fatigue duty to atone for our past pro-British sins, said yet others. We did not have much time in which to gore probabilities to unbloody deaths. We had to get ready for our own meeting with destiny.

We did not rule out the probability of our houses being stripped during our absence by looters recruited from the riff-raff of the other communities. The more enterprising among us collected the items which in our opinion would constitute the irreducible minimum of our worldly possessions, made them up into bundles and shouldered them. Alas, quite a few of us had to shed burdens too heavy for our unaccustomed shoulders, and our careful packing and bundling was a boon to casual pickers-up of such unconsidered trifles.

All had to go, irrespective of sex, age, or condition of health. The late Cheng Hui Ming, an interpreter at the Secretariat for Chinese Affairs, was among those who went to the concentration camp at Jalan Besar. The place reminded him, he said, of settling locusts or hiving bees. He had a friend in one of the houses in the concentration area. This man sheltered him and his family. Others not so fortunate had to encamp anywhere, in back-lanes and five-foot-ways, or in the open.

In these seething masses of humanity, some tempers were sure to be short. There was a free fight in one spot. The Japanese Military Police restored order and sliced off the ears of the combatants. The effect was magical.

The tension was relieved by a humorous side-show put up by the *Kempeitai*. One of their informers pointed out a man who had once worked for Tan Kah Kee as a mechanic. This man's hands were tied together by a rope; the free end of the rope was fastened to the seat of a motor-cycle, and the motor-cycle was started. As it gathered speed, the mechanic had to run faster and faster, finally to stumble and fall and be dragged along. The sight of a man frantically running a losing race with a motor-cycle was a welcome change for the *Kempeitai*, relieving the tedium of their severer duties.

Moving among us were Formosans, detectives and informers and renegade Communists who were purchasing safety by agreeing to pick out one-time associates. A crook of a finger by any of these acolytes, and a sacrificial victim was provided. How diligently we examined our consciences during those days of wrath! Whom had we injured, whom had we offended in the spacious days of peace? We composed our features, so as not to show any sign of resentment at the receipt of insult and contumely, or of indignation at the sight of insult and contumely received by others. They were the days of our searing. The days of our shearing would come in due course.

Unrealised by us at the time, we were being initiated into knowledge of an outstanding trait of the Japanese character — its love' for the haphazard, for improvisations. The average Japanese was contemptuous of deep-laid schemes, of long premeditation, of the children of 'silence and slow time'. He was so consumed by an ardent admiration for the deed done that he did not care for the way it was done nor for the why it was done. The way the concentration camps were run exemplified this love for the haphazard. There was no general system; there were no cramping rules of procedure. A commandant did as he saw fit. He did not fight shy of responsibility, no, not he. He and every one of his subordinates had the power of life and death. He and they accepted their godlike position without a tremor. They were equal to their duties.

One concentration camp lasted six days, another six hours. At one camp, over a thousand were detained, according to the survivors. At another, a small one, none. In some cases, the picking was thorough and conscientious; in others, perfunctory. For instance, in one case, the men were told to walk off. They scattered in various directions. Those who happened to go off in one particular direction were put aside.

The men of the following categories, however, stood in especial danger:

1   All who had had anything to do with the China Relief Fund, the real purpose of which had been the provision of 'silver bullets' for China's war of resistance against Japan.

2   Rich men, who, presumably, had given most generously to the Relief Fund.

3   Adherents of Tan Kah Kee, a veteran leader of the community and an indefatigable organizer of the Fund.

4   Newspapermen, schoolmasters, high school students, whose compeers in China had rendered themselves highly obnoxious to the Japanese by their antagonistic attitude.

5   All natives of the Island of Hainan, who, according to the Japanese, were Communists, every mother's son of them.

6   Newcomers to Malaya, those with less than five years' residence, who, presumably, had left China after the Marco Polo Bridge Incident, and who must have left China for one and only one reason — dislike of the Japanese.

7   Men with tattoo-marks, who, according to the Japanese, were all members of secret societies.

8   Volunteers, Volunteer Reservists, members of the Dalforce, all who had fought against the Japanese and might wish to do so again.

9   Government servants and men like Justices of the Peace, Members of the Legislative Council — men who were likely to have pro-British sympathies.

This did not mean that all the men of these categories were weeded out. Far from it. Nor did it mean that all who were weeded out belonged to these categories. The Japanese were not as efficient as all that. They did their best. But they were dealing with the 'Heathen Chinee',

16

past masters in deception and with no inclinations for inconvenient, unnecessary confessions. Many a wanted whale slipped through the meshes of the Japanese net and many a minnow caught in them were not those the Japanese really wanted.

Once the *Kempeitai* tried a ruse and it came off. It came off because they were dealing with Straits-born Chinese, whose native sharpness had been blunted by an English education. Would all Volunteers please put up their hands? Not a hand went up. "Ah, but you gentlemen need have no fears. No harm is intended. We desire your better acquaintance, that is all." One hand went up. The *Kempeitai* fell on that honest man's neck. What a grand fellow he was! They placed a chair for him, they told the crowd that he was a man after their own heart and that only such men were worthy of the honour the Commander-in-Chief had in mind, of entrusting them with garrison duty in Singapore, while the Imperial Forces went further afield. Thus adjured, a dozen men put up their hands. They were put into a truck and sent away, their exemplar with them. That was the last thing known of them.

On the fourth day word went round that women and children and men over sixty would be immediately released. Soon we saw the procession of these filing out with funereal slowness.

The rest of us were keyed up with expectation of our own speedy release that afternoon. It came to nothing, however. For we remained that evening and that night and the following morning cooped up as before. Our release did not come until the afternoon of the fifth day.

Then was a sight of thousands of people on the move, all heading for the exits. We were herded by men of the *Kempeitai*, who used the butts of their rifles freely, as well as clubs and sticks, to curb our impatience.

About five hundred of us had spent the days of concentration in a wired-in basketball court. The *Kempeitai* combed out forty or fifty of us and allowed the remainder to go out to join the main body. One of us was among the group of those detained. He felt weak at the knees, his palate went totally dry and he could hear his heart pounding, as he saw more and more of his less unfortunate companions going out by the door in the wire netting. After what seemed an eternity to him, he heard a growl from a Japanese sergeant. What, was the growl directed at him? Yes, it was. He joined the ranks of the spared and went out, the whole world a blur.

From the air the slowly moving mass of us must have looked like a black chemical retort with a long, slender, tapering neck. For as we neared the sentry-post, our last hurdle, we were ushered into a long single file, for questioning, one by one. A crack on the head was an infallible sign that one was wanted. Standing upright in a car outside and playing with a long bamboo pole was an officer who ran an appraising eye over us and, with a flick of the bamboo, designated the men whom he wished to honour. Receiving the accolade, the men stepped out, accepting the invitation to the dance of the doomed.

Ah! We were on the right side of the gate. Digging our finger-nails into our palms to master the over-mastering excitement, we shambled to a table ten yards away and bowed low ‘as we were presented with a piece of paper, one-inch square, upon which was stamped the word 'Examined' in Chinese. In days to come that slip was worth its weight in radium. It conferred a modicum of immunity on its possessor.

It did not give immunity to one of our number, however. No sooner had he arrived at his wife's house than he was roped in to a second concentration camp. He survived the second concentration, too.

In some camps the *Kempeitai* did not bother to prepare and issue slips of paper. They merely stamped the word 'Examined' on the arm or shirt of each man issuing from the camp. In the days that followed wearers of the decoration were hard put to it to preserve intact and visible the impression of that stamp, many going so far as to abstain from their accustomed ablutions for days on end.

Of those detained and not heard of since, the oldest was twenty-eight and the youngest twelve.

4   Habeas Corpus

What happened to those who were detained after the rest had been allowed to leave the concentration camps?

We did not know. Rumours were rife, each more frightening than the other. We in Upper Serangoon after the sixth milestone abstained from pork for a time. It was rumoured that pigs had been seen gnawing away parts of human carcasses grubbed up from shallow pits in the swamps of Ponggol.

In an island off Singapore the children of a refugee family, playing on the beach, day after day saw bodies washed ashore, some well-dressed, many tied together in threes or fours.

Days passed into weeks, and the weeks into months, and our missing ones did not turn up. We buoyed ourselves up with the hope that they were alive, working somewhere for the Japanese, and that the survivors would one day return to us. Months afterwards, when the Allies had landed on the Solomons, this hope received a fillip, for it was rumoured that an Allied broadcast had announced the recovery of a number of Malayans in Guadalcanal.

We could not believe that the Japanese could have done away with thousands upon thousands — how many thousands we could not say. It seemed so senseless a proceeding. We did not know that when Nanking fell, one hundred and twenty thousand were butchered.

Now, thirty years afterwards, after the holocausts in Baifra, and more recently in Bangladesh, one must marvel at the moderation of the Japanese in their dealings with us. Did they kill thirty thousand? They could have killed ten times that number.

In the weeks after the Fall of Singapore, we Chinese had an additional cause for anxiety. What was to happen to us? We heard rumours that the Japanese had been advised to move us pestilential Chinese to some large island near by, to let us starve to death.

I myself have no personal knowledge of what went on at a concentration camp. An Indian friend, proprietor of a Private English School, told me afterwards that he was at the time working for the Japanese, and that he had told the Japanese C.O. in our area that he knew the Chinese in Flower Road were 'good people'. Thanks to the late Daniel Sundram, we in Flower Road were spared the ordeal of the concentration camp at the seventh milestone, at which among those detained were two brothers, teachers in an English Mission School. Their mother was blind. Their brother, also a teacher, was in another concentration camp, and is alive today. I attended his son's wedding dinner two years ago.

I do not know when the members of the Chinese Company of the Singapore Volunteer Corps were ordered to report, whether it was before or after the concentration camps. Those who reported were not heard of again. Among them was an ex-pupil of mine, son of a washer-woman. He sold vegetables as a boy in the morning, before going to school, won a scholarship to Raffles College, taught in Raffles Institution, and in his spare time studied for an External Degree of London University. After getting it, he was awarded a Queen's Scholarship to Cambridge. He was due to go to England when the Japanese attacked Malaya.

Among those who did not report were two friends of mine. They got off scot-free. They are still with us.

Japanese ways were not the ways of common mortals. Their minds moved in a more rarified sphere than ours. They did away with the rank and file of the Chinese Volunteers, but spared the officers.

5   On Changi Beach*

I was a Singapore Government servant.

I was among those who went to the Jalan Besar Concentration Camp. At three o'clock in the afternoon of the fifth day, an announcer, probably a Formosan, shouted to us in the Amoy dialect to step out, those who were government servants and clerks in European firms. As a government servant, I stepped out.

We were told to form fours and march in the direction of Victoria School. About half of us had entered the school-gates when a Japanese officer ordered the rest of us to halt and squat down. About two hours afterwards, we were told to get up and resume our march. We entered the school grounds.

A fleet of military trucks appeared. A Japanese soldier had a bundle of thin Manila rope ready-cut for use. We were told to stand up and put our hands behind us. After tying our hands, he motioned us to board the trucks. There were about twenty of us in each truck, and there were about twenty trucks.

Our trucks started and moved off. There was no conversation among us. I thought we were being taken away for work of some kind.

*By Mr. Cheng Kuan Yew.

As Changi Prison hove into sight, one of us remarked that we would know the inside of a prison. But it was going to be much worse for us. Our trucks passed the gaol and turned to the right, and stopped at the beach. We were told to get down. As we got down, we were tied in droves of eights or tens or more, according to the lengths of the disused telephone wires the Japanese had cut for the purpose. We were next told to move off towards the beach. I saw a pillbox erected on the sea-wall of a demolished bungalow, and in the slit of the pillbox one or more machine-guns.

When the lot of us were all on the beach, about 400 of us, the machine-gunning started. I was at the end of my drove. As my companions were hit, they fell down and pulled down the rest of us. As I fell, I was hit on the face, I didn't know where.

The machine-gunning stopped. The soldiers came round to bayonet us. I shut my eyes. A soldier stepped on me to bayonet my neighbour. He did not turn to bayonet me. I shut my eyes and kept them shut. I heard the sound of trucks driving off. I opened my eyes. Night had fallen. There was moonlight.

A lump of coral was lying a few inches away from me. I worked my way towards it. I could move a little, being at the end of my drove. I rubbed my wire against the coral. It hurt my wrists, but I persisted, and finally got myself free of the wire. Next I rubbed the rope against the coral and soon freed my hands. Crawling on my knees, I glanced round. I saw that many had been bayonetted on the chest. Some were still alive.

I waded away from the pillbox. I was exhausted after a hundred yards or so. I made for the beach and worked my way across some barbed-wire entanglements. I struck inland and came across a drain. I had a long drink. I came upon an empty pillbox. There I passed the night.

The next morning I struck inland. I heard rifle shots. Were the Japs after me? The ground was uneven. I was in an abandoned plantation. There was much undergrowth.

I found a latex-cup. Breaking it against a tree, with a large bit of it I scooped out a shallow bed for myself. I lay in it and passed my first day. At dusk I came out of my hiding-place and followed a footpath. It led me back to the ditch of the night before. I heard shots and dogs barking. Were the Japs after me? There were bushes near by. I ducked into one and remained there until I heard the sounds of a departing truck or lorry.

The moon had set. It must have been near midnight. I got out of my bush, intending to make for the beach. I lost my way. I gave up and slept in a bush. Next morning I was awakened by the noise of the removing of benzene drums. I was near an oil dump. The removing lasted the whole day. I did not dare to leave my hiding-place. Thus passed my second day. I was faint with hunger and thirst. Flies were settling on my wound. And near by was the maddening noise of that day-long removal of oil drums.

Dusk came, and with dusk cessation of that maddening noise of oil drums. I crept out of my bush and made my way to the beach. I got into the water and, half-wading, half-swimming, I worked my way towards town. I bumped against something. A man came out of a bungalow, holding high a hurricane lamp. I lowered myself into the water, leaving only my nose out of the water. My nerves had gone to pieces. I retraced my steps and found myself at the mouth of a drain. After a drink from it, I stumbled along in what seemed to me a wilderness of barbed-wire entanglements. Finally, crawling into an empty pillbox, I slept the sleep of exhaustion.

Next morning I looked out. I saw some huts. Two Indians came out of one. A road was in sight. There were no Japs about. With the sight of the road, there dropped from me my long obsession of trying to get to town by way of the beach. Why should I not make for home by a land-route?

So I started. I went into a deserted bungalow. I examined myself in a mirror. I washed my wound in pipe water.

When the sun was high up, I arrived at a point near Changi Prison. I saw a group of British soldiers resting under a tree. I approached them. I told them that I had gone to visit a relative, and that I had been fired at, the bullet grazing my nose. The soldiers looked at me. One of them gave me a biscuit. Seeing me munching it, they said my wound was not serious.

I was led to an officer. He gave me a pencilled note. He told me I was on the main road. I should stop the first ambulance I might meet and give his note to the driver. He gave me a raincoat to sit on while waiting for the ambulance.

The ambulance took me to Raffles Institution, which was then used as a field hospital for the Indian Army. There my wound was dressed and I went home.

6 Alarums and Excursions

On the afternoon of Wednesday, 11th February 1942, I took my family to the Canossian Convent in Middle Road. I told the Reverend Mother that I was not a Catholic. Could she see her way to give my family asylum? She told me my family was welcome. There were hundreds of refugees on the ground floor of the Convent. No questions were asked about their religion. She insisted on my remaining with my family.

On Friday afternoon, I learned that there was a boat ready to evacuate women and children. I took my family to the wharfside. At the gate was a soldier with his tommy-gun on the ready to keep out the men. I begged him to let me in so that I could carry my family's luggage. I told him I would come out after seeing them to the boat. "But would you?" he said sceptically. So I left my wife and children to struggle along with their luggage.

I returned to the Canossian Convent to ask Grace's teachers who were there if they would care to take the chance of getting away. Two of them said they would. I took them to the wharfside and saw them through the gates.

The account that follows is the story of Grace, my wife, of her experiences after leaving Singapore.

N.I. was not allowed to come through the barriers to help us to carry our luggage. We had to struggle along with them ourselves. Nancy, the oldest, was only twelve or thirteen. We reached the 'godown' where the other evacuees had gathered. We had not been there more than half-an-hour when I saw Miss Sie and Miss Hu, two of my Chong Hock School teachers, coming towards us. How glad I was to see them! They explained that N.I. had gone back to the Canossian Convent to ask the Chong Hock School teachers there if they would like to take the chance to get away. The others had refused.

An air raid came on. A bomb must have fallen near us. Miss Sie put a pillow on her head. A splinter fell on it. There were some casualties.

Our ship drew near to the wharfside. We were told to show our departure permits. My party did not have them. Then we could not go on board, we were told. I told them that N.I. was a government servant and a member of the M.A.S. (Medical Auxiliary Service). They still shook their heads.

All those weeks I had prayed that if it was God's Will that we should leave, there would be no obstacles in our way. My prayers were forgotten at that time. At the gate there had been an obstacle placed in our way, and here was another. But what could I do? If I returned to the barriers, I would not know how to find my way to the Canossian Convent. So I begged and begged to be allowed to go on board. Someone in authority said to the man who was barring our way: "All right, let them go up!" So we climbed up the gangway.

Hardly had we stepped into the ship than another air raid came on. The ship rocked badly. We fell on each other in a heap. Ruth, then eight or nine, was at the bottom. When we picked ourselves up, she was white in the face. A Chinese sailor offered us the use of his cabin. It had two bunks in it. Ruth and Son and I occupied the lower bunk, Nancy and Ethel the top bunk. Miss Sie and Miss Hu slept on the floor. That night we were among the few people who slept in cabins.

Next morning, when we woke up, we found that the ship was not moving. We learned that the sailors had gone to an island near by to get branches with which to camouflage the ship. We were all ravenously hungry. Miss Sie and Miss Hu went round foraging for food. They returned carrying a large tray full of rice and corned beef. I made them sit down on the cabin floor and I ladled food into their mouths, like a mother bird feeding its young. We made a hearty meal.

After our meal, the children went out of the cabin to look round. Near our cabin they saw sailors taking out lifebelts. They told us to help ourselves to lifebelts and helped us to put them on, and they tied them securely for us. I found my lifebelt very uncomfortable and was about to untie it when I heard the cry: "Planes overhead!"

Bombs fell. We heard screaming and the rush of feet on the deck above us. People rushed madly for the ladders and the lifeboats. I told my children to sit on the floor of the cabin and pray, repeating the words: "A thousand shall fall at thy right hand and ten thousand at thy left hand, but it shall not come nigh thee." We heard explosions and screams on deck. We went on repeating those words.

After some time I went on deck. The panic was still on. I returned to the cabin and we went on repeating the verse of the Psalm. A European woman came and joined us.

I went on deck again and again after that, only to return to the cabin. I was waiting for the commotion to subside. The last time I went on deck, I found it almost empty. I told the children and the teachers to come on deck. They told me afterwards that they had seen dead bodies and parts of bodies. I did not see anything myself. The whole ship was on fire, except the part where we were. It was growing unbearably hot. I told the children to choose — fire or water? They chose water. Ruth held on to Miss Sie. I held Son's hand. Nan and Ethel looked after themselves. Nan was the first to jump into the sea. Then Miss Sie jumped in with Ruth. Next Ethel jumped in and Miss Hu followed. Seeing them all in, I pushed Son in, and then jumped in myself. I tried to cheer them up by telling them we had a beautiful day for a swim.

I saw many other people in the water. Few had lifebelts on. They were clinging to planks and floating wreckage. Wind and current carried us away in different directions. My party managed to keep together, except Nan, who was nowhere to be seen. Ethel cried for Nan. I told her Nan had gone ahead of us.

After some time we saw a lifeboat. Ethel shouted: "Nan is in that boat!" Nan also caught sight of us. She asked the people in the boat to row towards us and pick us up. They told her the boat was already full. Nan wanted to jump in and join us. They relented and promised to pick us up. As the boat came near, a young soldier jumped into the sea and helped us to clamber into the boat. No sooner had he got into the boat himself than he saw a wooden cask floating in the water. In he jumped again to get the cask. It might contain wine, he said.

Nan told us afterwards that she had been helped onto a floating mattress by a young Australian soldier, who propelled it by kicking out his legs vigorously. They had been picked up by the boat. So, humanly speaking, it was due to Nan that the rest of us had places in the boat, while many others, equally unfortunate and no less deserving, had to be left to the mercy of wind and waves.

There were thirty-five of us in the boat. Two men bled to death and their bodies were thrown overboard. I remember seeing a European woman doctor with a gash in her thigh who took her turn in rowing.

Three planes were flying low over us, as if about to drop bombs on us. We all crouched at the bottom of our boat which, unrowed, rocked dangerously. I prayed. I do not remember what words I used. But I prayed. Something made me say suddenly: "Don't be afraid. They may be American bombers." Hearing these words, my companions straightened themselves and asked me: "Shall we wave to them?" I replied: "Better not. But let's get on with our rowing." They picked up their oars, and resumed rowing.

The planes flew over us a few more times, back and forth, but did not drop any bombs on us, nor machine-gun us. Ours was the only lifeboat left.

Our progress was slow, overloaded and under-manned as we were. Towards evening we landed. Our leader, whom we called Capt. Ross, broached the cask the young soldier had retrieved. It contained water. Capt. Ross doled out part of the water to us. A Eurasian nurse gave her portion to her old, blind mother, who was enormously fat. She tried to coax my children to sleep next to her mother to keep her warm. Normally a poor sleeper, I slept soundly that night.

Next morning we went exploring. It was an island, small and uninhabited. We collected the few coconuts we found floating in the water, got the men to open them and we distributed the meat among our company. Capt. Ross again doled out a little of the water, starting with the youngest. A plane circled round the island, machine-gunning. Our boat had betrayed us. We hid ourselves among the trees. After the plane had gone, Capt. Ross sent the boat away. He stayed behind himself.

Among us was a Chinese doctor. He had twenty thousand dollars on him in currency notes. They were all in ten-dollar notes. He sunned them on the sand.

There was no stale coconut meat left for us to distribute. I went round with my children and the teachers looking for giant snails, which we smashed and distributed. Some made wry faces. I forced them to swallow the stuff. A bird dropped a small fish the size of one's hand. This I cut up into small pieces and gave them to the men. My son had the head and bones to suck.

On the third morning, while it was still dark, I thought I saw a figure in white, standing in front of me, which said to me: "Don't be afraid. Help is coming." What help, I did not know. Not long after, a *tongkang* came into sight. We shouted in order to attract the attention of the people on board. The boat drew nearer, but soon drew away. They told us afterwards that they had thought they were dealing with ghosts. Capt. Ross said that it was no use our going on yelling. But I would not give up. I got the Chinese women to wave their white panties together and to shout in unison in the Amoy dialect: "We are Chinese. Help us. Good heart gets good reward." The last sentence is the literal rendering of a tag which is often on our lips when we want to urge someone to do a deed of kindness.

We were heard and understood. The *tongkang* drew nearer and anchored. A small boat which was able to carry two or three persons was lowered. There was one man in it. He rowed towards us. When he landed, I explained things to him and asked him to help us. He said he would have to return to the *tongkang* and report to his captain. I should go with him and talk to his captain, he said. Capt. Ross agreed to my going, but would not let any of my children go with me. So I went on board by myself. I told my story. They told me they would take away all the Chinese. The Europeans would have to be left where they were, for fear of Jap vengeance. I pleaded with them and they finally agreed to take all away. I was rowed ashore, explained things to my companions, and the ferrying began. When all of us were aboard, we were given a hot meal of rice-gruel and salt-fish.

The *tongkang* was on its way home to Ek Chai, a fishing village. The men told me that there was a man in Ek Chai who was famous for his good deeds. He would take care of us.

When we arrived, we found the whole village waiting to receive us. Tears were rolling down their faces. They were so sorry for us. We were dispersed among the houses of the village, given food and clothing. After a few hours' rest, Capt. Ross said he wanted to go on to a place where he knew there was a hospital. He was given the loan of a *tongkang*. He thanked me, and asked me to thank the *tongkang* men and the men of the village for their kindness. He had not imagined, he said, that Chinese people could be so kind. He left with all the Europeans and Eurasians. The nine Chinese remained in Ek Chai — my family, Miss Sie and Miss Hu, and an old woman with her grand-daughter. The old woman claimed relationship with me and attached herself to me. She died about fifteen years ago. Her grand-daughter is the mother of children. Miss Sie also died fifteen years ago, of cancer. Miss Hu is hale and hearty, thanks to her practice of her form of Chinese 'boxing'.

Our host, Mr. Heng Hak Jin, was a dealer in charcoal, firewood and salt-fish. He was well-to-do, but by no means rich. *Heng* means 'king'. His generosity was on a kingly scale. He practised the 'religion pure and undefiled' of stretching out both hands to people who needed help and whom he could help. His wife was a willing participator in his deeds of mercy.

A few days afterwards, a Eurasian came to Ek Chai. He told me that he represented the British Government, for whom he was collecting all evacuees. The children screamed out: "We don't want to go. We want to stay with Ah Pek," meaning Mr. Heng. Miss Sie said she did not like the looks of the Eurasian.

But how could I put on Mr. Heng the burden of supporting the nine of us, and for how long? I did not know whether N.I. was alive or dead. Mr. Heng cut in. Hadn't I learned my lesson yet, that it did not pay to throw in our lot with Europeans? He told me I should remain where I was, among Chinese people. When I argued with him, he banged on the table. As his name was 'Hak Jin' (learning virtue), I and mine should not leave his house until N.I. came to claim us or sent word for us. As for food, he had bags and bags of rice, and when the rice was finished, he could draw on his store of 'paddy', unhusked rice. If it came to starving, his family would starve first, before he would let my family starve.

My mind thus set at rest, I told the Eurasian I would stay where I was.

Mr. Heng had business friends in Singapore. When communications were restored, he told me I could write a letter to N.I. and his friend would try to deliver it.

We stayed with Mr. Heng for nearly forty days, until the Japanese 'pass' came and enabled us to return to Singapore.

The children cried bitterly at having to leave Ek Chai and Mr. Heng whom they called 'Ah Pek', which is the honorific we Chinese give to someone who is older than our own father.

7   Adventures of a Worm

Having disposed of my family, I made for the head-quarters of the Zen society near the Uniteers building in River Valley Road. The incessant screeching of Japanese shells made sleep impossible that night. Next morning I went up to the first floor and sat cross-legged on a cushion and tried to meditate. A shell tore through part of the roof. The rubble fell on me. All my fellow-members were on the ground floor. Months afterwards, when I revisited the place, some of them told me that there were dents in the plaster of the wall before which I had been 'sitting', marking out the outline of a figure in the meditating posture. I cannot vouch for the truth of the story. By the time I went to the place again, the damage had been made good. Some said the phenomenon was a miracle in my favour, and some that it was a warning to me, a Christian and therefore a renegade, not to poach on the preserves of Confucianists and Taoists and Buddhists.

That night, Saturday night, and on Sunday, there was no let-up in the shelling. It stopped at 5 p.m. on Sunday. The silence that followed was halcyon, paradisical. At dawn on Monday, I went to my car and made for home six miles away. I had the road all to myself. No other car, no other human being. Coming down the slope before the Paya Lebar Police Station, I saw a roasted cadaver sprawling on the road. Just like a sacrificial pig, I thought.

My house had not been looted. I went to Bo Seng's house, thinking that his family might have returned, too. I found a Sikh installed in it. He snarled at me and I made myself scarce.

Next I went to Bo Seng's family house a mile away. Mrs. Bo Seng and her children were not there. No one knew where they were. It was fortunate for me that I had made my visits so early that day, for in the course of the same day, barricades were set up by the Japanese. All cars were confiscated.

A Eurasian lawyer, now dead, a fellow-resident of mine in St. John's Hall, Hong Kong University twenty years before, had parked himself in this neighbourhood. He had sent his wife away in good time. He sported a large hand-band bearing the legend in Chinese characters, which the Japanese called *Kanji*, that he was appointed a leader of the Eurasian community. Thanks to this, he was able to move about freely. Nightly, on returning, he regaled us with tales of what he had seen and heard. Chinese heads on Anderson Bridge, for instance.

One day, my Eurasian friend told me that he had news for me. All the boats that had left on the night of Friday, 13th February, had been sunk. Of the survivors, he said, the younger women had been picked out to serve as comfort girls for the Japanese military. Some of these, he said, were housed in the cinema theatre close to the Joo Chiat Market.

I made my way to Katong on foot, passing a number of barricades, each manned by a Japanese sentry. I saw men who had been kept back. They were slapped and kicked. I was a very sick man, and I looked like one. I bowed very low. I was allowed to pass.

I walked past the theatre a few times, looking furtively into the theatre. Then I turned into the lane beside the theatre. Someone in one of the houses recognised me and invited me in. He asked me what I was doing there. I told my story. He assured me that there were no Chinese women or children in the theatre. He advised me to go home. Well do I remember the lively sympathy shown me by the Eurasian mother-in-law of my Chinese friend living in that house.

So the days and nights passed for me, sick with fear that mounted with the stories my lawyer friend brought home at the end of each day. That I had suspicions of his deriving some pleasure from seeing me squirm, goes to show the unhealthy state of mind I was in at that time.

At that time, among the Straits-borns there was a sense of grievance against us China-borns. They had had no share in our anti-Japanese activities, and they thought it most unfair that they should have to share the hatred of our Japanese conquerors. Why did the Japanese not sort out the goats?

One day I learned from my lawyer friend that we Chinese had to pay a collective fine for our past misdeeds. Fifty million for the whole of Malaya, ten million for Singapore. 'The Overseas Chinese Committee' was made responsible for the collection of the money. The Goh Loo Club, a club for millionaires at Club Street, was made the headquarters of the Committee. It decreed that Chinese with landed property had to pay 8% on the value of their property.

I made my way to Club Street, sick in body and in mind. I met my old friend P. who was on the Committee. I poured my tale of woes into his ears. He cut me short by telling me that he, too, was separated from his family. But they had gone away in good time. In those days, with rumours flying round of the devilries of the *Kempeitai*, the Japanese Military Police, men had little sympathy to spare for whiners.

I filled in the form handed to me and declared that my land was worth $4,000, and in due course paid my share of the fine. I could have saved myself that money. Later on I learned that many braver people, small fry like me, had just ignored the call and got off scot-free.

Day after day passed without my having the least inkling of my family's fate. I assailed heaven with my tears and my cries. I scurried from place to place, wherever I thought I had the remotest chance of getting news. I would walk the six miles from Upper Serangoon, stop at a house in Weld Road, to let Grace's cousin, Mrs. Chong, know I was in town, so that she could put me up for the night. From her I received the greatest kindness. Her regiment of sons scoured the town for news for me. I spent the night in her house, and next morning set off for home, sick at heart. I would remain at home until I grew frantic again with anxiety and had to set off for town again to hunt for news.

Then one day Mrs. Chong sent one of her sons to tell me that someone from Ek Chai, an island in the Rhio Archipelago, was asking for me. I should call at a shop in Upper Boat Quay for news of my family. I hurried to town, found the shop, and was given a letter, which was indeed from Grace, in which she told me that the whole family was safe. Their host, Mr. Heng Hak Jin, a dealer in firewood and salt-fish wanted me to go over and join my family. He would take care of us. If I did not want to do that, then I should get a pass for nine persons, to enable her party to return to Singapore.

I went to Grace's very good friend Ruth, whose husband, a Formosan then in the employ of the Japanese, was able to procure the necessary pass. I was reunited with my family after forty days.

The story I heard from Grace's lips made me glad I had not been with her to cramp her style. It had been her finest hour. In those hours of dire peril, all her powers of mind, soul and spirit were concentrated on a point. She had burned with a blue flame, like an acetyline blow-lamp. Her children owed her their lives a second time.

8   Lim Bo Seng — I

Bo Seng was one of my early pupils in Raffles Institution, in 1925 or 1926. Yusof b. Ishak, destined to be first President of Singapore, was one of his classmates.

There was a girlishness about Bo Seng. He told me that he had never cut the throat of a fowl in all his life. He was tall and slim, and had a springy gait. He was shy, and at one time he blushed as easily as a girl. His voice was pitched lower than the voices of most Chinese. When he was crossed, it rasped. As a lad, he told me, he was the leader whenever any mischief was afoot. But at night he was very subdued. He feared the dark. Whenever he had to go to the latrine, he would pounce upon an unwary nephew or brother, tie the victim's hands behind him with a rope and, keeping a sure hold on the free end, hale him along to keep him company, occasionally tugging at the rope to make sure he was not abandoned.

Bo Seng went on to the Hong Kong University. But after two and a half years, on the death of his father, he had to return and, young as he was, he had to shoulder the burden of running a financial concern that included two brickworks and a biscuit factory, as well as an export and import business. He was head of his father's family numbering over a hundred persons, among them elder brothers, adopted sons of his father, some of whom proved thorns in Bo Seng's side.

Mr. Lim Bo Seng (right)

During the last few years of his life, Bo Seng's father's business had been going steadily downhill. When he died, Bo Seng, as the eldest real son, not adopted, took charge of the family concerns as chief trustee. His cleaning of the Augean stables was not popular. But the results were soon apparent. The leaks were patched up. Money-losing side-lines were wound up, like the wholesale import business of Australian wheat. Attention was focussed on the two brickworks and on the biscuit factory. Ever resourceful, Bo Seng improved the quality of 'Hock Ann' products all round. Soon the family business was running smoothly and profitably.

Bo Seng and his immediate family occupied part of one of the three houses in a large compound. With over one hundred people living in those houses, difficulties were sure to arise. In 1934 or 1935, Bo Seng decided to move out. He took over the larger of my two houses, separated from each other by a large monsoon drain. It was in that house that 'Bo Seng lost one of his daughters, a girl not much older than one year and hardly able to talk. She was lying in her cot with her glass milk-bottle. She rolled over and fell on the floor, cutting the bridge of her nose. I took her to a hospital where the wound was sewed up beautifully, the European surgeon saying that her beauty would not be marred by a scar when she grew up. Bo Seng went to see her. She clung to him and mentioned her nurse's name reproachfully. In the course of the night she died. Bo Seng took the loss very much to heart. He doated on little children. No sooner was one able to toddle and prattle than he longed for a successor to its helplessness. Had he lived, he would have proved as prolific as his father. As it was, he had eight children in the course of ten years.

With the family business firmly established, Bo Seng turned his attention to ways and means of making provision for the future for his immediate family. It was about this time that he acquired a controlling share in a granite quarry, from which his wife and children have derived a portion of their income in the post-war years.

He was modest and unassuming. But there was a glint in his eye that made it impossible for anyone to forget the steel hand in the silk glove. What man or woman of action could be without a touch of ruthlessness?

With me he was easy-going and never less than kind. We were friends, not business associates. I have never known anyone with his capacity for work. He seemed able to hold a dozen reins in his steady hands at one and the same time. I do not remember ever seeing him in a panic.

But there did come a time, I think, when some of his enterprises escaped his vigilance. He himself had a delicate sense of honour. But some of his associates did not. One of them was a man with a milk-white complexion who possessed a glib tongue. There was a ring of building contractors engaged largely in doing defence works for the British Government. A British Army officer was suspected of conspiring with contractors to swindle the British Government. The Police played in court a sound-recording of a conversation in which Bo Seng's handsome friend boasted that he had the British authorities in his pocket.

At this time Bo Seng had a haemorrhage of the lungs. He moved to a house at the seaside. He bought a large piece of land within five minutes' walk of my house and he started building his own house. When he was sufficiently recovered, he moved back into the house belonging to me, from which he could supervise the building of his own house. When it was ready, he moved into it. His wife is still living in it.

We shared a dislike for the 'pure-blooded European'. Bo Seng's European contacts were wider than mine and more varied. I only knew the bullying European. He knew the corrupt European as well. Some of the stories he told me of European venality made me gasp. How little I knew of the ways of the world outside the classroom! I was like the frog at the bottom of the well seeing a little of the sky and imagining it was the whole.

We both had, however, a just appreciation of the specifically English qualities of mind and soul that were the salt of the British administration in this part of the world, for instance, a sense of justice and a seemliness in the conduct of public business.

As a leader of the rich Amoy community, Bo Seng played an important part in the collection of money for the China Relief Fund.

The Japanese owned a large iron mine on the east coast. Bo Seng engineered a strike of 5,000 *coolies* working there. When these were replaced by Indians, he got to work through an Indian and called out these too.

These and similar activities made Bo Seng an embarassment for the local Government, anxious not to provoke the Japanese. Bo Seng told me that at one time he was in danger of having a banishment warrant served on him. But Mr. Tremlett of the Singapore Criminal Investigation Department was finding Bo Seng useful in helping to ferret out Japanese underground activities.

Later on, after the Japanese landing at Kota Bahru, Bo Seng helped to organise a labour force of 10,000 for work all over the island. He showed me an old-fashioned pistol which was all that Mr. Tremlett could give him.

Bo Seng was pro-Kuomintang and anti-Communist. But in these activities he was working hand in hand with the Communists.

I do not know when it was that Sir Shenton-Thomas asked Bo Seng to form a 'Chinese Liaison Committee' to assist in civil defence. I remember my mentioning to Bo Seng my wish to have my family evacuated to India. He told me that he had opened a list for his family and the families of his associates at the Emigration Department, to give them priority in evacuation facilities. He asked me to join his Committee. My family could then go on the list. He knew me well enough to know that I could not be of much use to him. But he wanted to do me a kindness.

41

The trouble was that the evacuation was delayed again and again, as more friends came to Bo Seng to have their families added to his list. In the end, there were 127 names on that list. His wife and my wife were the only women who could speak English and they were held back for the sake of the rest. Had they but left a week earlier, they would have had a good chance of reaching safety.

I have often marvelled at Bo Seng's iron will in carrying on his subsequent activities, knowing his family's danger. For the Japanese, as for the Chinese, a man's family shared his guilt and was liable to suffer for it.

I remember attending one meeting at an enormous bungalow opposite the Goodwood Hotel. It was presided over by a Brigadier Simpson.

On the morning of Wednesday, 11th February, Bo Seng returned from a meeting with the Governor. He had been told to leave at once with his associates. He handed to me a letter signed by Sir Shenton-Thomas in which he wrote that I had rendered the Government special service and that he called on all British authorities, civil, military and naval, to render me every assistance. Bo Seng had similar letters for his other associates. He told me we would have to leave our families behind. I told him that I would stay behind to take care of my family. I had no brothers to leave them to. Bo Seng agreed. He gave me $1,000 to keep for his family. How well I remember the stricken look on his face as he said good-bye! He looked like he was having another haemorrhage. That was the last I saw of him.

Mrs. Bo Seng and her children were taken to St. John's Island by a cousin of hers. He was a quarantine doctor. There they remained for the next two months, while the Japanese were combing Singapore for them.

The day after the Fall of Singapore, or the next day, Bo Seng's family house was surrounded by Japanese soldiers. There were actually three houses in the same compound. There must have been more than a hundred persons in them. Among them was a Taiwanese woman, wife of one of Bo Seng's brothers. She spoke to the Japanese officer in command. Hearing her speak his own language so fluently, he gave her a hearing. She pleaded with him not to punish them all for the misdeeds of one. Moved by her appeal, he contented himself with taking away fifteen grown-up men for further questioning. Of these, eight eventually returned. Nearly all were English-educated. The other seven were never seen again. They were all Chinese-educated.

A man may out-live a thousand sorrows or a thousand joys, but that is all a fairy-tale to a listener. Our lives are real for ourselves alone. To the young people of today, what happened thirty years ago may seem but a tale told by an idiot, signifying nothing to them.

9   Milking of the Chinese Cow

Within a week of the Fall of Singapore, the *Sin Chew Jit Poh* was resurrected as the *Syonan Jit Poh*. Three-quarters of the space was taken by the notification of the 'Military Administration Department' (M.A.D.); the remainder was given to items of news of an alarming import for Chinese generally. "Tan Kah Kee caught in Java." "Kao Ling Pai, Chinese Consul-General, drowned in the Java Sea." "X. executed for his connection with the volunteers and Y. for his connection with the China Relief Fund." The last item of news brought their hearts into the mouths of all the considerable Chinese leaders, for Y. had been but a minnow, not a whale, of the China Relief Fund. If he had to die, who could hope to live? They scurried away into hiding. Thanks to the Formosans, they were all ferreted out.

According to the *Syonan Jit Poh*, Dr. Lim Boon Keng was the only surviving Chinese leader. He was said to have been rescued by the Imperial Army from the firing line, where he had been abandoned by the British. What Dr. Lim, a septuagenarian, was doing in the firing line was a question that only a few had leisure to ask themselves. The truth of the matter was that the *Kempeitai* had spotted him among the Chinese in one of the concentration camps. They put it to him that he should come out as leader of the Chinese community. Dr. Lim who had been living in retirement, full of years and honours, as a former Member of the Legislative Council of the Straits Settlements and later on as President of the Amoy University, naturally demurred, pleading as excuse his age and infirmities. The Japanese showed him the utmost consideration, honouring his white hairs. But Mrs. Lim's hair was not snowy white. In the end, through the intervention of Shinozaki, the old couple were released and sent home, a *Kempeitai* agent in their wake. Dr. Lim could not resist this solicitude and finally yielded, assuming the mantle of Leader of the Chinese of Singapore.

The first instructions soon came. Dr. Lim was to form a tentative interim committee. He succeeded in mobilising a brace of doctors, a lawyer, a couple of compradores and a few businessmen, and filled up the gaps by roping in two of his former pupils in Amoy.

On 27th February Dr. Lim was instructed to report at the Goh Loo Club — rendezvous of rich men. There he met a very subdued lot of men. One had donned a monk's robes and was fumbling with his beads, another was shivering like one having a bout of malaria. All but one had come out of Japanese cells, where they had tasted, in varying degrees, Japanese kindness. They owed their rescue to a Formosan, Wee Twee Kim, who was present in all the glory of a Japanese uniform. Wee Twee Kim addressed the meeting. He told them that a few days after the invasion of Malaya had started, there had been a mass meeting in Tokyo at which a resolution had been unanimously carried — to beg General Yamashita to exile all the Singapore Chinese to an uninhabited barren island and let them starve to death there. Singapore, according to them, was a hotbed of anti-Japanism and the people were guilty of the crime of helping to finance China in her resistance against Japan.

Upon whom should the righteous anger of the Japanese nation fall, if not upon the Chinese of Singapore?

His hearers went paler yet. No one in that otherwise so voluble company opened his mouth. Silence grew oppressive. Men looked into each other's eyes and saw despair. At long last the Formosan murmured a suggestion or two. There was a nodding of heads and the following proposals were framed and adopted unanimously:

1   To call a mass meeting to pledge loyalty and obedience.

2   To 'provide comforts' for the troops.

3   To send delegates to convey to the High Command these loyal professions.

The delegation waited upon Lt. Colonel Oishi, *Kempeitai* chief. Wee Twee Kim the Formosan was interpreter. Lt. Col. Oishi asked them to speak freely. But no one opened his mouth. At last Mr. T. mustered sufficient courage to beg that all Chinese detained during the concentration might be released. One of his sons was among them. When this request was interpreted, Lt. Col. Oishi flew into a rage, banging the table. What right had they to proffer requests, he demanded. He drove them from his presence.

They were not to have a second interview for a considerable time afterwards. They were left to stew in their fears. Meanwhile, they were receiving daily accessions to their numbers, as more and more men were released. These had their baptism of torture. Messrs. T. and O. who had taken refuge on a neighbouring island were arrested after their return and given their quota, but they came out of it alive. The manager of an amusement park was less fortunate. His family was guilty of criminal negligence in giving in ignorance 'tea-money' to the agents of the *Kempeitai*, instead of to the agents of the Special Branch, and he was flogged to death by the irate Special Branch, who felt themselves robbed of the fruits of their labours, for he had been caught in a net of their spreading.

There was at the time a rift also among the Chinese generally. The Straits-borns had a grievance against the China-borns. They had not trafficked with Chungking. One of their leaders had years before coined the phrase 'King's

Chinese', and they had lived up to it. Who was Hecuba, and what was Hecuba to them? What sums they had given to the China Relief Fund had been paltry, and given only under compulsion. Shinozaki, a Japanese who had been serving a sentence in Changi Prison for espionage when Singapore fell, played up to the Straits-borns and took them under his wings, pluming himself as Protector of the Straits-borns and the Eurasians, while the Formosan Wee Twee Kim, once a store-keeper in a Japanese firm in Singapore and now a hanger-on of the Japanese military, posed as the friend and protector of the China-born Chinese.

After the Japanese Military Administration had been set up, the leaders of the Chinese community were summoned to an interview at the Fullerton Building, now renamed the 'Gunseibu'. They were kept waiting for a long time. At last came a short stocky Japanese of a dark complexion, his upper lip adorned by a moustache looking for all the world like a tooth-brush. His name was Takasei. Actually he was a very minor figure in the Japanese hierarchy. But how were they to know? To them he was as awe-inspiring a figure as Genghis Khan ever was. He said sternly: "You are our enemies. You know this. You have fought us for years. Now you know our strength, don't you? Your activities undermined our position here. You helped the scoundrelly British. Now we've got you. We shall have to put you where you'll do no more mischief. Now, what have you got to say?"

Said the Chinese spokesman, stammering: "We have come, Sir, to pledge support to the Japanese Military Administration."

T.:   What support do you mean?

C.S.:   Those with money, give money, those with strength, give strength.

T. (stormily):   *Bakaro!* Your money, and even your lives are ours to use as we please. Get out! Go home and think how you're going to expiate for the crimes of your community.

The delegation retired sheepishly.

The next day, through the good offices of their Formosan friend, the Chinese delegates were graciously given permission to call again.

T.:   Well, what do you want?

C.S.:   We most respectfully inform Your Honour that we propose to place our lives and our wealth at the disposal of the Military Administration. We await orders.

T.:   Good! Your answer is more to the point than yesterday's. I'll inform the High Command. Now go and think over the question of how you are going to make good your offer.

The third interview took place a few days afterwards. It was Takasei again who received them.

T.:   What have you got to say now?

C.S.:   We've come to receive your orders, Sir.

T.:   I have no orders for you. We don't want to confiscate your wealth. But have you thought how you're going to set about it — to give us your wealth, as you said you would?

C.S.:   We offer up half our wealth to the Military Administration now, and will hold the remaining half in trust for the Military Administration.

T.:   Very well, I'll transmit your offer to the High Command and give you their reply in due course.

Thus ended the third interview. Then followed days of anxiety. Day after day they repaired to the Gunseibu, to see Takasei, and he would not vouchsafe them a glimpse of his godhead. In the meantime, the air was heavy with direful tidings. Town after town in Johore was dispeopled of Chinese, as they were slaughtered wholesale. T.S.L. and O.P.T. as well as many other rich men were again haled away by the Special Branch. Screams of tortured men increased in volume at the Central Police Station, at the Y.M.C.A. at Oxley Rise, and at other *Kempeitai* centres.

Said Twee Kim the Formosan: "You, the so-called Chinese leaders, have shown no real signs of repentance. I cannot go on helping you. I must warn you that the future is full of dark possibilities for you and for the Chinese generally."

More days passed. All Chinese in town, and many in the suburbs, learned the depressing news in the course of those days. Was a second concentration contemplated, to be followed by a general massacre this time? We looked at one another and saw despair. What could we do? What offer could our leaders make? We waited in dumb despair for whatever might befall.

Under these louring skies there flashed a summons for our leaders. We drew in long breaths and let them out again. The gods and our Japanese masters were perhaps relenting. For one day in March, at three in the afternoon, the Formosan Twee Kim came to the Goh Loo Club and told our leaders assembled there that the Chief Administrator would immediately receive them at his residence in Nassim Road. They went at once. There were fifty of them. They were ushered into a large room where they waited, all standing. There were two chairs in the room, but none had the temerity to sit down. After more than an hour, Colonel Watanabe, the Chief Administrator, came, accompanied by Takasei. Col. Watanabe sat down and was a silent witness of the proceedings. Takasei addressed the Chinese delegation:

"I am a Confucianist. My family has worshipped Confucius for six generations. I pay the most scrupulous regard to the claims of benevolence and justice and all the moral virtues. I have your welfare at heart. Knowing what severe punishment would be meted out to you by the

Imperial Forces for your past crimes, I have hurried here from Tokyo to try and save you. I have been in Malaya three times. This is my fourth visit. I used to meet some of you at O.B.T's house. You ignored me then, some of you. You didn't know me then. Now you know me. I am a recognised authority on the South Seas and I realise what part you Chinese have played in Malaya. Now you say you place yourselves and your wealth at the disposal of the authorities. Good. I am glad to see that you do appreciate our goodness and respect our regime. But, remember the Imperial Forces do not ask for your money. What I am going to say is a personal suggestion from me, engendered by my friendship for you. I suggest that your community make a gesture of submission and a goodwill offer of fifty or sixty million. I on my part will use my influence to prevail on the Commander-in-Chief to accept it. I shall also urge him to give you protection and release your properties which are now held by the military. It is unnecessary for me to remind you that you have given Chiang Kai Shek billions, that you have allowed the British to use you and that you have often threatened the lives of the Japanese living here. You have not yet given any token of sincere repentance and you deserve the most condign punishment. But I am anxious to help you. I hope you appreciate my kindness."

This speech was translated into the Amoy dialect (Hokkien) by the Formosan.

Our leaders bowed very low and took their leave, unexpectedly unburdened of the terrors that had oppressed the whole community for days past. Our masters would graciously accept ransom for our lives. It only remained to hammer out a scheme for raising the money. It looked easy enough for a rich community like ours. Why, the Loke family of Selangor and the Eu family of Singapore alone could pay the ransom for the whole community and not be reduced to beggary! But a banker reminded them that at the time of the British collapse there was only 220 million in circulation, and here was a demand for a quarter of that!

Considerably chastened, they went into the question of electing a committee. They called it the 'Committee of the Overseas Chinese Association of Singapore', and not the 'Peace Preservation Committee', as in China, where the puppet organisations were so styled, and elected as chairman a person who was privileged by virtue of his past tenancy of a cell in gaol as a Japanese agent. This man now blossomed out as the Dictator of the Overseas Chinese, the other committee members being either his jackals or his very obedient servants, serviceable men, who were duly respectful and did not say over-much, unless at his own direction.

The first duty of the Committee was to allocate the sums the different states had to contribute towards the grand total of fifty million dollars. Singapore's share was ten million, Malacca's five million.

Sub-committees were formed to deal with the sections in our community — a 'Hokkien Sub-committee' for the people from the Fukien Province, a 'Teochew Sub-committee' for the people from Swatow, made up of representatives of various localities, men conversant with the financial standing of all the men likely to be laid under contribution. Forms were sent out or applied for. No defaulter could plead failure to receive a form as excuse. We were supposed to apply for forms if none reached us. The rate was 8% of accepted value of property. The owner of a house valued at three thousand dollars had to pay $240, for instance. When these forms came back, they were passed on to the Investigation Sub-committee. Precautions were taken to forestall corruption and favouritism. The items declared were scrutinised by examiners of a section different from that of the declarant. For example, Hylams scrutinised the forms of Hokkiens, and Teochews scrutinised the forms of Hylams. These items were next compared with the records of the Land Office and the Income Tax Office. Finally a notice was sent to the declarant specifying the sum due from him and directing him to pay into this bank or that. The accounts were checked every second day by the *Kempeitai*.

The month of grace passed and Singapore had collected only three-tenths of her contribution. Even the President of the Association, old Dr. Lim, had not paid up his $2,000 as he had no money. Takasei summoned the Committee. He was furious. They were a pack of liars, of nincompoops, men of no initiative and no energy. He had the representative of the Straits-borns locked up as a lesson to the others.

Representatives of the Overseas Chinese Associations of the different states were summoned to Singapore and conveyed there in military cars. There they were roundly scolded, adjured to be more zealous and expeditious and sent packing the same evening. The Malacca representatives tried to tell the Japanese authorities that it was manifestly beyond Malacca's power to pay 5 million dollars, as she had had only $1\frac{1}{2}$ million dollars in circulation when the British abandoned Malacca. They were invited to go and see the Chief Administrator, and when they arrived there, they were promptly arrested.

Now the representatives of a certain state were late for the meeting, having been delayed by a little business of their own. They were not so unworldly as to let slip a chance to do a spot of black-marketing, while they had the use of military conveyance for a day or two. When they started from home, they had intended to raise objections. But the moment they learned of the arrest of their Malacca friends, they forgot all those objections and bolted for home.

On 20th April, a check-up was made. The amount collected was still short of the amount demanded. Takasei was furious. Anger came to him easily. He foamed at the mouth. Peremptory orders were sent out to summon representatives of the various Overseas Chinese Associations a second time. They met at the Goh Loo Club. His scowling face boded them no good. He reminded them that the offer of a paltry 50 million dollars had originally come from them. What did they mean by not dishing it up now? They did not have the money, did they say? They were liars. Down came his fist on the table. "Penang, what have you done?" Penang jumped. Recovering, she asked for an extension of time. Extension! Why, he had given extensions galore. "And Malacca?" he next yelled. Malacca asked if she could give rubber and gold to make up the balance. And Singapore, what had Singapore to say for herself, demanded Takasei. Dr. Lim, in a voice trembling with emotion, said that he and his associates were no liars. When they promised the 50 million, they meant it. The delay was due to financial conditions beyond their control. They had done their best and if they had to die, die they must. And his voice firmer by this time, he concluded, "I wish to point out, however, that the manner in which the Government is raising this contribution is without a parallel in any country." He sat down and wiped his eyes.

Whether the Formosan ever gave a faithful rendering of the old man's speech or not was never known. The youthful old man had spoken his mind and yet lived!

On 20th May representatives of all the Overseas Chinese Associations of Malaya met in Singapore again. Twenty-eight million represented the sum total of their labours. They waited for the worst.

The manager of the Yokohama Specie Bank was the *deus ex machina*. He offered the Chinese a loan of 28 million dollars payable within a year at an interest of 6%. The Chinese were saved.

The Chinese were told to prepare a beautiful casket to hold the cheque for the fifty million and a loyal address. The formal presentation was fixed for the morning of 25th May. The address had to be approved by the Military Administration first.

At midnight the Formosan went to Dr. Lim's house. The wording of the address was not acceptable to the authorities, he said. Dr. Lim went to the Japanese Headquarters with the Formosan, returning at 2 a.m. with the amended address. Eight more visits were necessary, however, before the address was finally approved. The meaning is as follows:

> "In the past we were running-dogs of British imperialism. We wronged the Japanese and helped Chiang Kai Shek in his criminal resistance to Japan. We now see the error of our ways and heartily repent. We pledge our support to the Military Administration. Of our own free will we offer the sum of 50 million dollars as token of sincerity."

One of the representatives demurred at the phrase 'running dogs', suggesting 'puppets' instead. According to him, 'running dogs' belonged to the category of mere beasts, whereas 'puppets' still bore some resemblance to human beings. He was overborne. The Chinese community had to style themselves 'running dogs' and drink the bitter cup to the dregs. We hardly dared to make a mouth even in the privacy of our own homes.

The presentation took place at three o'clock. Sixty representatives foregathered at Fullerton Building, in the chambers of the defunct Chamber of Commerce. A huge Japanese flag was on the wall. There was a platform and on it a rostrum. Below the platform were two chairs.

The Chinese representatives rehearsed their parts in the coming show. The rehearsal over, they waited and waited, standing. Old Dr. Lim fainted and had to be given water to revive him. After more than an hour the Commander-in-Chief appeared. Looking very grim, he stalked to the platform. Col. Watanabe, the Chief Administrator, and Takasei took their seats in the two chairs below the platform. Beside them stood the Formosan Wee Twee Kim and the Japanese Ando, interpreters. The Chinese stood at the other end of the room facing the platform. Dr. Lim, supported by the Presidents of the Selangor and Penang Associations, stood a few paces in front of the rest. At a pre-arranged signal the three presidents went three paces forward. The man on the right gave Dr. Lim the address, which he read, Ando rendering it into Japanese. The three presidents advanced three steps more. The one on the left handed to Dr. Lim the cheque which Dr. Lim offered to General Yamashita, who graciously accepted it. The three men bowed low and stepped six paces backward, returning to their original places.

General Yamashita gave a speech lasting more than an hour, in which he delivered an eloquent dissertation on the causes of the war and on the moral and spiritual ascendancy of the Japanese race, who were the descendants of the gods, he reminded them. The Europeans, on the other hand, were monkeys as Darwin had proved. If there was war between gods and monkeys, the great soldier triumphantly concluded, even a fool could see who would win.

A few days afterwards the *Syonan Jit Poh* published a crucial announcement of policy towards Chinese in the Southern Regions. "The Chinese in the Southern Regions occupy a reasonably important position. From now on the Imperial Government must govern them with severity tempered with benevolence."

Thus was the Chinese Cow milked.

10   Co-prosperity

We were dwellers in the Japanese 'Co-prosperity Sphere'. As was fitting, we had the 'Co'; the Japanese had the 'Prosperity'.

Mommotaro is a fairy-tale included in the second reader for Japanese schools and has for many generations past leavened the minds of millions. To the foreign reader it is interesting, as it throws a flood of light on the inner workings of the Japanese mind.

Mommotaro was the foundling of an old couple, childless and poor. When he grew up, he left home to go in search of fortune. He was no visionary; he was no knight errant. He didn't tilt at windmills. He made for the castle of a giant reputed to possess fabulous wealth. The giant vanquished, Mommotaro spared him, graciously accepting his treasure as ransom.

Japan must have appeared to her sons and daughters as the Mommotaro of the nations. They are descended from the Moon Goddess. They owe a duty to their divine origin: they must shed abroad the light of civilisation on the benighted nations of the world. If in the process they are enriched by the treasures of the nations they benefit, what could be more fitting?

The history of Japan has been unique in that she has never lain prostrate at the foot of an invader. She has always given, she has never taken. Her islands have always remained 'Isles Inviolate'. Not that she has never made war. But war — war against neighbouring nations — has always paid rich dividends. Now, the war in Malaya was no exception, for when they succeeded in prying open the Malayan oyster, how they must have licked their chops at the sight of the heaped-up treasures exposed to their view! The equipment and supplies of the vanquished foe were theirs, as were also the goods belonging to enemy commercial firms.

Singapore was filled to bursting with goods. She had supplies sufficient to last her and the hinterland for three years. Moreover, she was still holding the supplies intended for Hong Kong and for Siam, for Indo-China and for the Malay Archipelago.

All these supplies were immediately seized by the Japanese as part of the spoils of war and would never be available for civilian consumption.

What about the stocks held by Chinese and Indian traders and kept in their shops and private warehouses? Now, compared to the amounts under seal in the godowns lining the miles of wharves, these stocks were pitifully small, but in the aggregate they were considerable. Would the Japanese allow them to remain in civilian hands? At the moment the Japanese seemed too busy raking in their gains to bother themselves about what was in comparison a mere bagatelle, and which, in any case, was safe enough, not having wings to fly away from the island.

All commercial dealings on a big scale had ceased. There was a shortage of money. The future was uncertain. Further, the Chinese financiers, capitalists and businessmen had not yet got over the effects of the concentration camps. They were too dazed to think of market manipulation.

Singapore witnessed the spawning of a new tribe of sellers — sellers of looted goods. The streets of Chinatown were white with them. They were anxious to dispose of their holdings. Rumour was rife that our conquerors would

57

deal with looters in a summary fashion. So prices were ridiculously low. Champagne could be had at two dollars a bottle; and for twenty dollars a man could amass a respectable collection of impressive-looking volumes at ten cents a volume. It was a glorious time for bargain hunters. But, of course, this trading was ephemeral, languishing and then dying of inanition, as supplies gave out.

Normal trading was resumed, as Chinese businessmen needed money with which to pay their contributions to the ten million dollars Singapore Chinese were liable for. Further, they seemed to possess sensitive antennae, for they had intimations of imminent moves on the part of the Japanese. So they were anxious to reduce their holdings to manageable proportions.

They were right. For the Japanese Military Administration soon promulgated a law regarding 'controlled goods'. These were to be sold at prices slightly higher than the prices prevailing before the Fall of Singapore. Dealers were required to declare their holdings. If any failed to declare or made false declarations, he would be 'severely punished'. Then no unauthorised dealing was allowed. A buyer had to get the permission of the Japanese authorities before he could buy. This order meant that certain commodities were withdrawn from circulation and put into cold storage, for future use by the Japanese. It had the added advantage of saving the authorities the bother of having to store and look after the goods in question.

Logically, dealings in these commodities should have ceased forthwith. But in practice things were not so simple, thanks to the saving graces of cussedness and lawlessness in human nature.

For not all holders of the prohibited commodities declared their holdings and of those who declared, many withheld part of their holdings. Thus, thanks to the courage and enterprise of these men, clandestine dealings were still possible and a modicum put aside for civilian consumption.

Business remained dull, however, in the Black Market as well as in the White Market. The reason was a shortage of cash. For the Japanese had not yet begun to pump money into the market. They had not yet begun to purchase goods. They were still gorged with loot. But with the progressive clearance of their war booty southwards to supply their forces as they went further and further afield, the Japanese began to have leisure to look around them, take stock of their position and gauge their probable needs in the future.

They began to enter the market as purchasers. They were generous. The prices they paid sometimes left us gasping. They became almost popular. It paid to deal with the Japanese. A young naval lieutenant, in conversation with a Chinese friend, said that the Navy did not mind how much it paid so long as it got what it wanted. This sensible policy had the immediate result of inducing a sense of optimism, as business revived. Men rushed here and there in a frantic search for goods to sell to the Japanese.

One man had lost everything at the Fall of Singapore. All his stock had gone as the result of looting by our own people or confiscation by the Japanese. He had not indulged in the unmanly pastime of counting broken eggs, but had gone into new ventures, tentatively at first, gradually gaining confidence as he went along. Eventually he was doing so well that when his family returned from Java, he assured his wife that he would yet make another fortune for her and her children. That brave man would probably have made good his boast if he had lived, but he died not long afterwards.

His optimism was part and parcel of the general optimism among all businessmen at the time. The period of depression and stagnation was over. There was money in circulation once again. There was buying and selling. At last the Black Market was in a healthy condition; it had the commodities, and it had the money. Prices began to rise. Operators made money. There was a general sense of well-being.

Among the Japanese there were a few who tried to stem the rising tide of inflation. For instance, the Registrar of Vehicles during the first year of the Occupation carefully scrutinised sales of motorcars. He insisted on interviews with buyers and sellers. Woe unto the seller who demanded what the Registrar considered an exorbitant price! He was slapped and kicked to persuade him to be more reasonable in his demands. One gathered, however, that his zeal was actuated not by anxiety over the effects of inflation on the local population, but by a wish to guard his fellow-countrymen against the greed of unscrupulous men.

Such pommelling, however heartily it was done, did not avail much to curb the Black Market, which went from strength to strength, encroaching on the domains of the White Market, as more and more commodities were placed on the list of 'controlled goods' and as the operators of the Black Market grew more and more familiar with the intricacies of their calling.

For the mass of ordinary people, as the spectre of inflation advanced, the reaction was simple. They went without. Cloth was prohibitive, let us say. Well, they gave up buying new clothing, patching and repatching the old. It was a sovereign remedy, going without, but its efficacy was narrowly circumscribed by other factors. As time went on and food supplies decreased, enterprising men started their manipulations and manoeuvres which rapidly induced a total eclipse of the normal channels of buying and selling of foodstuffs. The markets were empty; window-dressing in shops became obsolete: the shops had nothing to sell.

The really lean period for the common people of this land dated from that total eclipse of normal commerce. Food grew dearer and dearer. They could not give up eating. Medicine grew dearer and dearer. To be ill or not to be ill — that was no question for them to answer. And the less food they had, the greater their dependence on drugs, as their reserves of strength and resistance to sickness steadily diminished. What could be done? The question gave many a man many a sleepless night. They could have wished themselves and theirs cooped up in the internment camps, where, if they went short, they could be sure of having something at least, and if they starved, they could starve in company with others, and be free from the reproach of supineness.

That was a real reproach. For if a man was hard up and had to subject his wife and children to privations and hardships, he was to blame, not Providence. The remedy was in his own hands. He could go into the Black Market. Easier said than done, however, for participation in the Black Market presupposed some capital, connections and aptitude, failing which he and his were condemned to a hard existence. To an ineffectual of this type the temptation to preen himself on his superior virtue came easily, but self-righteousness was a mighty poor substitute for full meals. And after all, it is always the lot of the irresolute to get left, though sometimes the process is called the will of God.

This door slammed in his face by natural disabilities, such a man would have to draw on reserves in the form of jewellery, furniture, piano and refrigerator.

The prices for these things were low during the first year of the Occupation. For instance, in May 1942, a radiogram was offered for sale for $400 which had cost $600 in October 1941, and there were no offers! But as the Japanese population increased, prices began to rise. For the Japanese, to our surprise, turned out to be as sybaritic as the rest of us, loving rich food and soft raiment.

A Japanese newcomer had to have a house. The house had to have furniture. This came out of the houses of the impecunious among us. The new Japanese establishment had to have a mistress to preside over it and see to the comfort of the master. This woman had to have trinkets dear to a woman's heart. These came from the wives and daughters of the impecunious among us, who were forced to sell possessions to live.

Prices steadily rose. A piano worth $200 in December 1941 was worth $800 in December 1943, $10,000 in December 1944 and $15,000 in June 1945. A Parker fountain pen worth $15 in December 1941 was worth $500 in March 1944 and a year afterwards, $5,000.

From this one might think that a man could keep himself and his family going for months by the sale of a few trifles. But the truth was, the prices of these things lagged far behind the prices of foodstuffs. Thus rice, which was $5 a picul in December 1941, soared to $200 in March 1944 and to $5,000 in June 1945.

Now, among the ineffectuals who would not or could not go into the Black Market as active operators, were men who in pre-Occupation days had been well-to-do. They had large reserves of jewellery. Thus, in their case, there was considerable ground to cover before they would reach the ultimate bourne of their solvency — the engagement and wedding rings of their wives. As for poorer people, it was but a hop, skip and a jump, and they had arrived at the end of their resources, and thereafter the question 'What next?' stared them in the face.

Should they let their daughters go out and work as waitresses (these had to be attractive and under twenty-one) or as ornamental fixtures in offices (the Chinese styled them 'flower vases') or as coolie-women in factories? Or, if they wished to spare their daughters, should they go and enrol themselves in the honourable company of informers?

An Anglican priest was visited by a parishioner, who handed him some money, saying that it came from the bishop. With it the priest was to procure wafers for the bishop to use at the Holy Communion. The priest was about to take the money when he remembered one of the last instructions of his bishop before going into internment — that should communion wine run short, water would serve the purpose. Remembering this, he refused to comply with the supposed request of his own bishop. Soon afterwards, he learned that the bishop was at the Y.M.C.A., a notorious *Kempeitai* centre.

Actually, blackmailing was more profitable than betrayal, the trembling victims paying far more than either police or *Kempeitai*.

When masters and mistresses were having such lean times, it was not surprising to find an exodus of household servants, even among those who had seen the children grow up, for they could earn much more by joining the 'queues' for cigarettes, for fish, for meat. 'Queueing up', in fact, became one of the major professions. When successful, the proceeds of the long wait could be disposed of at ten times the sum paid. Thus many a household drudge of the old days was far better off than her one-time mistress.

Our own servant-girl refused to leave us. She would work for us for nothing, she said. She remained for more than a year, until her grandmother found her a good match. Now, thirty years afterwards, the good, kind Ah Lam is the mother of half-a-dozen grown-up children and on her way to becoming a grandmother herself. She is one of the simple souls who helped to keep the race sweet.

In the old days many of us in Malaya had thought that the Chinese had a monopoly of corruption — that these imps of Satan knew neither honour nor honesty and that they had practised venality so assiduously and for so long that they would almost try to palm-grease St. Peter himself. When the Japanese got to work, however, what an eye-opener it was for us! The Chinese had found their masters. They had to hide their heads in shame. For the Japanese were beating them at their own game.

In justice to the Nips, one must admit that they had reason to admire their own moderation — that able to take so much, they could be content with so little! The basic reason was, of course, the impossibility of converting their ill-gotten gains into yens, to support the dignities and iniquities of a budding noble house.

Our Nip masters introduced us to *kumiais* — a new word for a new thing. In Malaya we had known only one monopoly — the 'Government Opium Monopoly', which impinged on the lives of opium-smokers only. Now everything was a monopoly. There was even a *kumiai* for charcoal and firewood, and a *kumiai* for nightsoil. We were hedged in by *kumiais*. We could not move an elbow without coming into contact with some *kumiai*. There must have been a *kumiai* for coffins, and a cynic expressed surprise at not finding a *kumiai* for marriageable girls.

The idea was to mobilise all available resources and harness them to the Juggernaut of Japan's war. The needs of her armed forces came first, of course. These fed off the land wherever they went, so that all the supplies it was necessary for them to bring were of a military nature in the strictest sense — guns and ammunition. As for food and everything else, these had to be provided by the conquered population — price of the 'protection' extended to them, which means, put very crudely, the returns they made for having been spared by their conquerors.

It was given out, however, that the real purpose of the *kumiais* was the mobilising of local resources to ensure equitable distribution among the local population. Hypocrisy is ever a tribute paid by vice to virtue. Robbers always claim to be benefactors. And it is a moot point which turns the gorge more, the robbery itself or the pious professions of the mealy-mouthed robber. One wonders whether the Japs ever had an inkling into the truth, how there was a smouldering resentment in the hearts of us all.

It is easy to see that after the Japanese armed forces had helped themselves to what they considered necessary for themselves (and for their jackals) there was mighty little left for the civilian population, and to make things worse, that little had to run the gauntlet of a host of agencies before reaching the intended consumers. There is many a slip between the cup and the lip. 'Consumers' is a misnomer, for mighty few of us did any of the consuming.

Conditions might have been less unbearable if there had been a sufficiency of rice for bare existence. But there was not. Starvelings are ever the best trencher-men.

Singapore was better off than many other places. Up to the very end, the rice ration was eight katties a month, which was half the quantity sufficient for sedentary existence. In some places the ration was less, in others there was none at all. For instance, the inhabitants of a fishing village nine miles from Malacca had only rations of two katties twice in sixteen months.

One was forced to the conclusion that our famine was man-induced, to compel us all to toe the line and serve the Nips. Supplementary rations and cigarettes were used as baits to lure us. Thus Government and Municipal employees had a supplementary rice ration of five katties a month, and employees of the military fifteen or twenty katties a month. It did look as if the Japanese were deliberately making us go short of our staple food, so as to secure a plentiful supply of labour for their purposes, and they were to some extent successful.

In the midst of this dearth and near-starvation, the Japanese were conspicuous by reason of their prosperity. They did not share our lot. They were raised high above our level. They had as much of the necessaries of life as they needed, all the rice and sugar and meat and fish they could consume. When home-fare palled, they could use the coupons that a solicitous government had provided for the purpose and go for a change of diet at a restaurant. Nor were they confined to these coupons. Whenever they had a fancy for anything, they had only to say the word and men tumbled over each other to satisfy their whims. Delicate viands like shark's fin and bird's nest were there in plenty to titillate their palates; whisky and brandy at five thousand dollars a bottle were conjured out of hiding places and 'State Express' cigarettes at two thousand dollars a tin of fifty. Their paramours could have Parisian perfumes and American lipsticks to beautify themselves with, and the children of these auspicious unions could have Horlick's Milk and Klim.

Whenever a Chinaman is most generous, he is most dangerous. His far-famed hospitality is at times merely a financial investment. What cared he if he had to spend twenty thousand dollars on a night's entertainment of two Nips if he could be the richer by a couple of millions in the course of the next few days?

Thus it paid to cast one's bread upon the waters when one was dealing with Nips.

A rich man was running a gambling farm. It was a gold mine for him. The craze ran like a prairie fire. Everyone, from the millionaire brewer to the *belacan* pounder's wife, had a stake on the day's number.

Now, that gambling farm would have had but a brief existence without the countenance of many Nips in high places. The proprietor made his way to the hearts of these by way of their stomachs, entertaining them sumptuously. Having made his way to their hearts, he had next to win them wholly, so that the machinations of unscrupulous rivals would have no effect. This did not take the wily old Chinaman long to do. He had a multitude of daughters — adopted daughters — for his agents scoured the town and environs for presentable girls whose parents were willing, for a consideration, to let him adopt them. The girls themselves were rendered malleable and pliable by judicious gifts of jewellery. He bestowed these adopted daughters on Japanese sons-in-law, thus rendering his position impregnable.

11   Pebbles for the Cairn

Richie Byrne was one of my last pupils in Raffles Institution, in 1937 or 1938. He was a harum-scarum fellow with a gift for repartee, and some of the recklessness and generosity of his Irish forebears. He and I escorted some women to a biscuit factory. The women went in to try and coax the manager to part with some biscuits at 'controlled prices'. Richie and I waited outside. As the 'five-foot way' was deserted, our tongues went clacking over the foibles of our Nip masters. Richie got married in January 1943. He was arrested in June, and met his end in November. Before his death, his pregnant wife had a message from him, asking her to name the child after him, if a boy. Richie was barely twenty-one when he died.

Lim Siew Tee was another pupil of mine at R.I. He did me many kindnesses in those dun days. From him I heard the story of how he saw a fleet of lorries full of P.O.W.'s, white men, half-starved and bare-bodied. From the opposite direction came lorries full of Indian soldiers, who had been reorganised as the 'Indian National Army' under Subhas Chandra Bose. They were now allies of the

Japanese. The Australians and the Indians passed each other by in stony silence. But at the end of the fleet of lorries carrying Indians came some lorries carrying Gurkhas. The Australians cheered the Gurkhas, and the Gurkhas cheered the Australians. Some boys who were peddling cigarettes caught the infection and, running alongside the lorries, shied fistfuls of cigarettes into them.

Half-way through the Occupation there was an exodus of people from Singapore. The luckiest ones moved to Cameron Highlands. The Japanese put no obstacles in their way.

My sister sent me word that I should move my family to Malacca. She had been there for ten years and had many friends there. She rented a bungalow at the seaside and laid in provisions. But I was possessed by an immense lassitude. Left to myself, I would have done nothing. But Siew Tee got the railway tickets for me, queueing up for them for two days with the help of a relief. He also managed to borrow a lorry to get our belongings to the station.

When I returned to Singapore eighteen months afterwards, there was no Siew Tee for me to thank. He had died in the interval from a defective heart.

A.C. Rajah was a young teacher in R.I. I admired his English style. In December 1941 he was one of four entrusted with the duty of producing a fortnightly propaganda paper for schools. Soon after the Fall, A.C. was nominated for the Propaganda Department. He had the temerity to refuse. For a year, however, he was refused an appointment as a teacher, and when he was given one, it was to a school many miles away from his house. Hardly had he completed a month's work before he was nominated for the Japanese Normal School, and this time he did not dare to refuse.

He hanged himself one night in the school latrine.

Tajudin Chunchie was my colleague at R.I. He was a cricketer, a wine-bibber and an amateur businessman. He was stopped at his efficiency bar year after year. He was a good teacher, but fate would always send someone to inspect him when he was off-colour.

One of his haunts was a Japanese hotel on the sea-coast commanding a fine view of Naval Base. Before commending myself to old Tajudin's tender mercies, I always took care to undo my tie, for he would grow emphatic after a few glasses of Asahi beer. One of his cronies was a Japanese doctor practising in Singapore.

In the middle of 1942, Tajudin came to see me in my house. He was as irrepressible as ever. He flaunted a pair of spectacles from which one lens was missing. He said that the Japs had offered him a place in their Propaganda Department, with which would go a car with a flag in its bonnet, as well as a fat salary. Tajudin dearly loved to loll in a car. But he turned down the offer. The reason he gave me was that as a Propaganda bastard, he would have to blackguard the British, who, poor devils, were having a bad time, and besides, he, Tajudin Chunchie, had eaten the salt of the British Government. He would not join in the popular game of damning the British.

All this he said with relish, in the way I knew so well, so characteristic of the man I had known for twenty years. He told me to keep my end up. The Allies were not doing so badly, he said. The British were sure to come back. He had access to some hidden radio set.

That was the last time I saw my friend. As a Malay, he could get away with much. But in the end he landed himself in a *Kempeitai* cell, from which he was removed to the hospital and there he died. I cannot vouch for the truth of that report. All I know is that Tajudin Chunchie did not survive the Jap Occupation.

To most of his fellow-teachers, old Tajudin was a buffoon. Little did they know that his buffoonery was a mask for deep feeling. Motley, my masters, was the only wear for a man like him. But there was stuff enough in him to stuff half-a-dozen mannikins, like me for instance, and yet leave a little over.

Hiroi was a Japanese private and graduate of the University of Tokyo. He was a frequent visitor at my house for two months in 1942. To me and my wife he spoke of his old father, a poetaster addicted to Chinese verse, of his wife, of his one-year-old son, and of his dog. He showed us a photograph of his wife and son. He and I had one thing in common — anxiety for the health of our wives.

He was a favourite with the boys of this neighbourhood, to whom he gave lessons in *Nippon-go*.

From Port Dickson he sent me a letter in English, sending it by a private, accompanying it with an English-Japanese dictionary which he had used in his student days and which his father had used before him.

Some months afterwards he sent me a postcard from Formosa, in Japanese.

Hiroi's friendship meant much to me. He must be among the Japanese casualties of the war. Otherwise he would have got in touch with me without loss of time, once the war was over.

Lee Ek Kiam was in Government Service as an Assistant Surgeon. Only Europeans could be Medical

Officers. Tired of being bullied even by the Nursing Sisters, every one of them a European, E.K. resigned and went into private practice. It did not make him rich.

E.K. refused to enter the Black Market for medical supplies during the Occupation. Patients went to his house. He went round to visit those who could not move about. He had his bicycle.

A Eurasian patient needed injections. His wife did not know how to get them and she had no money. E.K. told her to set her mind at rest. He would get the injections — and never mind about the money. He could rob the next rich patient who came his way, he said.

The woman reminded him that she and her husband were not friends of long standing, nor were they members of his church. E.K. brushed these objections aside with an airy wave of his hand.

E.K.'s shadow seldom darkened the door of any church.

I was a friend of long standing. On me and mine he showered countless acts of mercy, especially on my sickly wife, delicate as cut glass.

E.K. died ten years ago, after a long illness, leaving his family badly off. Recently I attended the wedding dinner of his daughter.

To E.K. I owe another kindness. I had a ravenous hunger for authentic war news, not the news excogitated by the egregious *Syonan Shimbun*. E.K. satisfied that hunger. Among his patients were some who risked their necks. One had a radio set in a laundry basket.

12   Kempeitai Kindness

The late Tan Thoon Lip was a fourth generation
Straits-born Chinese. His great-grandfather founded the
Tan Tock Seng Hospital. He attended English schools. He
won one of the coveted 'Queen's Scholarships' which took
him to Cambridge. He was taken into the Straits Settlements Civil Service after graduation. He was familiarly
known as T.L. He read no Chinese, and only spoke a little
Hokkien, the dialect spoken by the people of Amoy. The
same dialect is spoken by the Taiwanese.

It sounds stuffy and Victorian to say that T.L. was a
scholar and a gentleman. But I can think of no other words
to express what I mean. He was a man of culture, many-
sided, and of impeccable taste. He never did a mean act
nor said a mean word. I have never met a man like him.
At times I thought he was too good to live.

After Singapore fell, T.L. was appointed head of the
local staff of the Office of the Custodian of Enemy (that is,
of British) Property. The Custodian was a Japanese named
Asahi, who had two other Japanese as his deputies, the
senior of whom was Wada. Asahi was soon transferred,
partly due to his unpopularity with fellow-Japanese. He was
too efficient, had a good command of English and had ways
that local people could understand. He was no uncouth

boor, as were so many of the Japanese, whose idea of maintaining discipline was to bark *Bakaro!* (Fool!) at the offender and give him a kick or a slap.

On 10th November 1942, T.L. was taken to the Central Police Station, to a room on one side of which was a lavatory occupying a quarter of the room. In it he found a Jap in uniform sitting on a table swinging his booted feet. He was in his shirt-sleeves. He had taken off his jacket and laid aside his sword. T.L. was to learn that he was Toyoda of the *Kempeitai*, the dreaded Japanese Military Police. In the room was a Formosan. Toyoda barked out something in Japanese. T.L. looked inquiringly at the Formosan interpreter, who snapped in Hokkien: "Kneel!" He repeated his command with some heat before T.L. could bring himself to obey. He had never before knelt before a man. He asked for someone who could speak English to interpret for him, as he was not fluent in Hokkien. Both Toyoda and the Formosan sneered. But they shouted for an English-speaking interpreter. With this man came also a Malay-speaking interpreter.

The room soon began to be filled with about a dozen people, Chinese detectives and informers who had learned enough Japanese to try interpreting. There were also two Chinese whom T.L. called Mr. A. and Mr. B., assistant torturers.

The Formosan, at a word from Toyoda, asked: "What is your connection with the Auctioneers, Ltd?" T.L. said he had none. Toyoda roared *"Pukul!"*, Malay for "Thrash him!" He picked up a leather strap some 4 feet in length and 3 inches in width and laid it on T.L.'s back a few times. He paused and repeated his question. Again T.L. said he had no connection with the company except in his official capacity, and that he had no shares in the company.

The next question was whether he knew Mr. W.? T.L. replied that he had known Mr. W. for eight years, and that he was a personal friend. "Tell us about him," Toyoda barked out. "What do you wish to know?" T.L. asked him. "Everything!" was Toyoda's reply. When T.L. said he did not understand, Toyoda rained blows on him. Interpreters and informers joined in the fun, shouting questions at him in English, Chinese and Malay.

Toyoda was tired and handed his strap to Mr. B., who used it with such vigour that Mr. A. stretched out a hand to restrain him. All this time T.L. was on his knees. Toyoda strode up to him and kicked him on the back and in the ribs. A well-delivered kick sent him across the room to where Mr. B. was standing, and Mr. B. expertly kicked him back to Toyoda. More questions were asked, followed by more beatings. T.L. was told to confess or he would get more beatings. It was useless for him to try to hide anything; they knew everything. T.L. begged to be told what he was charged with, what he had to answer for. No, he was told, that was not the way the Japanese did things. That might have been all right under the British, but under the Japanese there were ways and means of making him speak.

Toyoda barked a command. A pail of water was brought into the room. T.L. was made to lie down close to the window. A chair was placed on his chest, the footrest just touching his chest and the legs preventing him from shifting from side to side. A heavy plank was laid on the footrest crosswise with his body. A hefty man sat on the chair. One man held his ankles together, another his wrists. Two men covered his mouth with a cheese-cloth. He was asked if he would confess. When he replied that he had nothing to confess, the cloth was stretched tightly over his face and water poured over his nose and mouth.

The 'water treatment' continued for a quarter of an hour or more, with intermissions for questions to be barked at him. He asked to be confronted with his accuser. He was told to stop thinking that he was still under the British, and that it was not enough for him to deny. They knew everything and they could make him speak.

At the end of this session, Toyoda made a little speech which was translated for T.L.'s benefit. "You are a government servant. We know your good reputation. You hold a high position and the various communities hold you in respect. You must not be stubborn. Your body cannot stand the punishment. If you will confess all your wrong-doings, I shall let you go. I shall reinstate you in your position. Well, what have you to say?" T.L. again said he had nothing to confess. This time he was not beaten. An English-speaking interpreter was detailed to take him to lock-up No. 3. A clock somewhere struck one. T.L. had been put to the test for two hours.

Session followed session with the same routine of questions and tortures. He was not, however, given the 'water treatment' again.

On the fifth day of his detention, T.L. had to face a new *Kempeitai* officer named Midzuma. This man began by saying that he knew T.L. had worked hard for the Japanese. He would get a free pardon if he confessed his faults and showed readiness to assist the Japanese administration. "You can go home tomorrow if you will tell us everything you know about Wada." T.L. realised that he had received all that *Kempeitai* kindness for the last four days not for what he had done or left undone. He had merely been 'processed' to make him willing to tell the Jap Military Police all that they wanted him to tell them about Wada.

T.L. said that he knew nothing about Wada's private affairs, and that Wada was in charge of immovable properties, while he himself had been in charge of movable properties. Midzuma pressed him with questions. Did he not know that Wada kept women, and that he had sold houses? T.L. repeated that he knew nothing about Wada's honesty or morality. Midzuma next asked him if Wada had had anything to do with the disposal of movable properties under T.L.'s charge. The reply was that Wada had recommended sales at prices obtaining before 8th December 1941, in accordance with a ruling of the Japanese administration. Each prospective buyer had come with a note from Wada recommending the sale. T.L. had instructed auctioneers in writing to value the properties and release the properties on payment. Asked if he knew if Wada had made money out of the sales, T.L. replied that he knew nothing of it.

On the seventh day, T.L. was again examined by Toyoda, who had Midzuma's notes with him. Wada was said to have sold nine hundred houses and kept the money, and T.L., as he was in charge of movable properties, must have been in the know. When T.L. repeated what he had said to Midzuma, Toyoda lashed him with his leather belt and kicked and stamped on him. He repeated that, as far as he knew, Wada had not taken any movable property without paying for it. This interview lasted one and a half hours.

To cut the story short, T.L. signed Midzuma's statement on the sixteenth day of his detention at the Central Police Station. He saw no more of either Toyoda or Midzuma after that. He remained at the Central. He records that every time a Japanese officer visited the place, all the prisoners had to kneel at the iron gates of their cells and remain kneeling until the officer's departure. The entry was heralded by a stentorian shout, as was also the exit.

Here we must digress and say something about Wada. According to T.L., he had lived in Singapore for many years and liked Singapore and her people. He had been infected with our habit of tongue-wagging, made possible for us by the British principle of freedom of speech. He had even dared to express a preference for the Singapore of British days and to criticise the Jap administration. His unbridled tongue must have had something to do with his undoing.

On 8th December 1942, T.L. was transferred from the Central Police Station to the Y.M.C.A., another *Kempeitai* torture-house. There he had only a short session with the

Kempeitai, during which he was not beaten. He had the benefit of a short lecture. He was told that he had been reborn into a better age and he must show his gratitude by assisting his benefactors in all possible ways. No one could live long in Singapore, he was told, without knowing something about other people. He should tell them who were the people in his office who should be weeded out. He should think things over and let him, the lecturer, know whenever he had something to say.

There were five cells in the Y.M.C.A. T.L.'s had eleven inmates. Among them was an Australian soldier named W. Hughes. He had escaped from internment with two comrades. They hid on an island and were fed by neighbouring villagers. There they remained for three months. One evening they were seen by a Malay fisherman. Next morning the place was surrounded by Jap soldiers with tommy-guns. Hughes did not know what happened to the villagers.

A middle-aged Chinese, silver-haired, who looked to T.L. more like a saint than a criminal, was brought in. He was a tuberculous diabetic. Within three days he was removed in a coffin. His wife cursed the Japs. Even the detectives and informers present pitied her. They warned her to be quiet. How would she like to have her teats pricked with pins and needles, a favourite Jap treatment for women?

At two o'clock in the afternoon of 8th January 1943, a Japanese Military Policeman came into T.L.'s cell with a list of names. T.L.'s name was among those called out. What more devilry did the *Kempeitai* have in store for him? His anxiety must have appeared on his face, for as he passed Wada's cell, he heard Wada whisper to him in English: "Steady. God will know."

It proved to be the first amnesty of the new year. He was one of seven to be released that day. But not without ceremony. They were brought into the presence of a

Japanese officer with gold braid in his tunic, who made the farewell speech, telling them their cases had been investigated and that the Japanese Military Police were satisfied that this was their first offence. A lenient view was being taken of their offence. They were being pardoned, and therefore should be grateful.

At the entrance hall, they were treated to another speech by another Japanese officer, who reminded them again of the magnanimity of the Military Police and who ended his homily by telling them not to repeat to any person outside what they had seen and heard. So ended T.L.'s ordeal, which had lasted from 10th November 1942 to 8th January 1943.

At a war-crimes trial of *Kempeitai* personnel, a Japanese witness for the defence said that the *Kempeitai* always had "prior knowledge of the crimes of any man brought up before them for questioning. If such a man did not confess, trickery was practised on him, and if that failed, we required a lot of time, but no violence was used, as it was the great motto of the *Kempeitai* that there should be no violence".

So T.L. and thousands like him had the consolation of knowing that what they had had done to them was not meant to be 'violence' and was merely 'trickery'.

The above account is based on T.L.'s little book *Kempeitai Kindness*. He died at a comparatively early age. He was one of Singapore's sons whom Singapore has a right to be proud of.

13   I was a Japanese Government Servant*

I worked at the Chinese Secretariat in pre-Occupation days.

Soon after my return from the concentration camp I was instructed to report for duty at the Economic Research Department.

The Japanese who interviewed me was a middle-aged man with a shaven head. To my bow he returned a nod. It did not take him long to find out what an ignoramus I was. I knew no economics, had never done any research, and did not know a word of Japanese. But he was not minded to be over-exacting. Could I run a library, he asked me. Having a family to support and badly shaken at the concentration camp, I was anxious to meet him half-way. I told him that I had had some experience as a student librarian in my college days, and I volunteered the information that I knew some French. He was interested for, he told me, he too knew French. My heart sank, for what French I remembered could not have exceeded two dozen words. Fortunately, he was in no better case, and so my French was not put to the proof.

So I became a librarian at the Economic Research Department. At the time of my appointment the library

*By the late Mr. Cheng Hui Ming.

was non-existent. But I was given two peons and authority to cart away all the likely books I could lay hands on. I had no difficulty in finding magazines, newspapers, etc., for most offices were deserted in those days. I have to confess, however, that my collection was largely made up of trash, but I had to justify my appointment.

I count it a great mercy to have been consigned to an obscure library, which gave me a public appointment of some sort and which served to shield me from the courtesies of informers as well as the zeal of those whose duty it was to impress people for the labour gangs.

So for three and a half years I was allowed to remain in my little niche, arranging, labelling and indexing my books. I acquired and put into practice the gentle art of malingering, of seeming to do so much and actually doing so little. I browsed among law-books, departmental reports and Government Gazettes covering the years 1880-1938 and thus came to realise how little I knew of the background of my duties as officer in the Chinese Secretariat.

After breakfast, in which tapioca was generally the staple food, I cycled to office. I was more fortunate than many of my colleagues who, not possessing bicycles, had to walk to office. At one time the Economic Research Department occupied part of the sixth floor of Fullerton Building. We had to pant up the six flights of stairs. The electric lift was not for the likes of us. It was reserved for the Nips.

Later on we removed to Fort Canning. In one way it was an improvement: we no longer had to climb six flights of stairs. In another way it was a change for the worse, for we had to run the gauntlet of Sikh guards, who punctiliously exacted from us the bows due to them as representatives of *Dai Nippon*.

Our routine duties started with half-an-hour's *Radio Taisho*, which, Anglicised, means mass drill, for which we adjoined at the ground floor. Our Nips set us the example.

They pitched in with zest. As for us, even with the best will in the world, we could not hope to emulate them, and went through the exercises perfunctorily and listlessly, wisely conserving energy. What we needed was not physical exercise, but more digestive exercise — more food, food that had as much roughage as tapioca and far more nutriment.

There was one tribulation peculiar to me. Our Nips used to assail me with demands for books and pamphlets not in my collection, which I was supposed to produce immediately. We had our share of peppery Nips. Woe was me, if I happened to have one on my hands any day! His ire rising, he would abandon English and jabber in Japanese, storming at me. To have tried to explain would have been adding fuel to the fire. So I bowed before the storm, interjecting *"Hai, hai"* (Yes, yes) at decent intervals until my Nip master, realising my denseness, would go away from me, and I could breathe again.

I was irresistibly reminded of myself in the days of my nonage standing sheepishly before my kindergarten-mistress and getting a thorough dressing-down.

A Nip, we found, was continually having fresh brain waves. No sooner did a new idea occur to him than he had to put it into effect. So we were continually trekking from one building to another. Whenever we moved, everything went with us, we left nothing for the incoming occupants of the office, not even a broken chair.

For a year the head-office was in Singapore. Soon we were reduced to a branch office, the head-office going to Sumatra, to Taiping, to Kuala Lumpur. The local personnel refused to budge, however, giving a variety of reasons, and fortunately our excuses were accepted at their face value. The Japanese flitted about; we stayed put.

Our first head of department was a lieutenant. He was a man of many moods, friendly one moment and fierce and forbidding the next. When he was friendly, he was garrulous. His fellow-officers were nincompoops, mere swashbucklers, without the most elementary notions of administration, he said. As for the generals, he said, they owed their rapid promotion to Chiang Kai Shek who had given them their chance in life, as well as their education in the art of war. The Malayan campaign was a vacation jaunt compared to fighting in China.

To all this balderdash I paid the politest attention.

This amiable specimen of the Japanese *Samurai* remained with us for four months. When he went, we had a group of officers in his place. We, the local staff, had to bow to every mother's son of them. For myself, I came early to office, and when the Japs trooped in, I was either in the latrine or in the library. In the evening I reduced my bowing to the irreducible minimum by staying on until the road was clear.

As a race, we Chinese are addicted to bowing. So it is surprising that we should have disliked bowing to the Japanese so intensely. But then our bowing is'so different from Japanese bowing. When we bow, we relax all our muscles and bend like willows before a gentle breeze, overcome by respect, genuine or simulated. When a Japanese bows, he stiffens all his muscles and bends smartly, like a marionette, his trunk at right angles with his legs. The stomach exercise involved is too strenuous for us indolent Chinese.

One group came from Manchuria. They were characterised by their contemptuous attitude and hectoring ways. They were not only seasoned warriors but experienced bullies. Fortunately for us, they were transferred to Sumatra when the head-office went there.

In their place came a group of professors. One of these, a Ph.D., was introduced to us as a 'financial wizard'. Poor man! He never had a chance of showing off any sleight of hand that I could see. Many a time I found him dozing in the office. A fellow-professor and rival sleeper was an authority on Social Science and had the enviable aptitude for sleeping anywhere, however hard the spot, in his chair, on an unused table, in the rubbish-room or on a narrow bench. A third professor (of Statistics, I think) had a weakness on which we, the local staff, played. Whenever we wanted a concession or a favour, our emissary was invariably a 'flower vase', and a good-looking one.

Another Jap (not a professor) possessed a delightful American accent and a stentorian voice. His main duty, it would seem, was to watch over our manners. Whenever he found us remiss in our bowing, he would roar at us, doing justice to his American accent and to his powerful lungs.

The Japs in the Economic Research Department were, as a body, to be pitied. Ours was not a money-making department. We cut no ice in the Black Market. So our Nips had no side-lines and had to be content with their rations and modest salaries.

Far be it from me to suggest that every Nip I worked under for three and a half years was either a cad or a buffoon. Some of them were gentlemen and would win the suffrage of any decent company. A man named Mizuno stands out in my recollection. He was no egotist, nor a jingoist, nor a bully. He carried himself with a becoming dignity and modesty. He never foamed at the mouth with hatred of the British, nor did he ever thump the table to awaken in us a due sense of the superlative excellence of Japan. There was never a word on 'Co-prosperity'. Never unduly familiar, he did not think it beneath his dignity to show courtesies to us, his subordinates.

My heart went out to poor Mizuno when I saw the stricken look on his face when news of the surrender of Japan became known.

This pathetic gullibility of Mizuno's was, I realised, characteristic of his race. It was indicative of the extent of their surrender to their leaders. That the leaders might prevaricate was too sacrilegious a thought to entertain even for a moment. Thus a Jap swallowed everything his superiors told him, however offensive it might be to reason and probability. One of our Japanese lavished much time and care on an ingenious diagram which showed at a glance the mounting losses of the Allies. One day in the latter part of 1944, I stole a look at it and was amused to learn that in the space of a week forty-seven battleships, twenty-one aircraft carriers and nearly four thousand planes had been accounted for by the *Kamikaze* airmen.

Our Japs did all they could to induce us to learn Japanese. Promotion would depend upon degree of mastery of the new language, they warned us.

They went to work with enthusiasm. 'Impossible' was not a word in the Japanese dictionary. Many of us had spoken nothing but English from our cradles. Many of us were too advanced in years to engage in new linguistic adventures. All these considerations counted for nothing, however. Their fiat had gone out "Let Japanese be spoken", and they fully expected it to be spoken. One fine morning they would rattle off in Japanese. We blinked, uncomprehending. They repeated. We again blinked. They would get into a fury. That did not work either. They soon gave us up for a bad job. Their own enthusiasm quickly evaporated. They relapsed into English in their dealings with us. We gladly met them half-way, adapting our own to theirs.

It was a truth universally acknowledged that Japan had one of the highest literacy figures in the world: nearly all Japanese could read and write. The figures for secondary schools must have been correspondingly high, and every secondary-school pupil learned two foreign languages. Hence many Japanese knew English. That few could speak it was not to the point. They could all read it. Their love for learning was impressive. Finding themselves in a library, they invariably made a bee-line for the most ponderous-looking tomes; they had no use of anything frivolous. They were addicted to translating, and their translations were inspired by a laudable zeal for exactness. "We must take British war news with a pinch of salt", Japanised, became "we must read British war news and eat some salt". One of our professors was nonplussed by the phrase "to draw the long bow" He consulted one of his Chinese subordinates. "Exaggeration," the man said. The professor's face was suffused with pleasure and gratitude. *"So-ka?"* he said. "It means 'exertion' *ka?*"

In one of the offices at Fort Canning some electric bulbs were stolen. The local staff were instructed to meet and listen to a homily, which ran as follows: "You know how serious is stolen to the Japanese. Five electrical globular objects lost in two consecutive nights in succession. We must now finger-print your five fingers in both hands. Very sorry to do this. But in Japan no stolen. We open doors at night." The finger-prints were duly taken and nothing more was heard of the affair.

The following is a gem of Japanese-English prose and can fairly be accepted as a specimen of the stuff they habitually produced for our delectation.

"Chinese in Syonan-to have hitherto been in sympathy with wild propaganda of Chungking Government, and majority of them supported the aforesaid government and taken politically and economically the same action with Britain against Japan and moreover they have positively participated in British army in forming volunteer military activities and still have recently disturbed the military activities of the Nippon Army as guerilla corps or spies and thus they have always taken anti-Japanese actions at their first front and it goes without saying that they, in spite of being Eastern race, were indeed so-called traitors of the East Asia who disturbed the establishment of the Great East Asia."

In a notice concerning ration cards, the following words occurred:

"In the event of that the change of address caused by the removal or the decrease or increase of occupants arose in the household, then the amendment with respect to the transition should be entered tersely into the census list at the respective head of team and also at the divisional Police Station."

It ended with:

"Anyone who obtained the purchasing card under false intent or pretence, or the wrongful interpolation or amendment made wilfully thereon, shall be severely punished."

We came to know that phrase, "shall be severely punished", rather well, for it was the close to every Japanese proclamation and notice.

Outside one electric lift was a poster bearing the tag "Japan fights for equality of Eastern races and also Co-prosperity" and cheek by jowl with it a notice "For officers only" (which means Japanese only). Every time I passed the spot I feared to find either the poster or the notice gone, but to my delight they remained in close proximity for as long as I can remember, the inconsistency seeming to have put no Nip out of countenance.

What a people! One could not imagine a Nip standing before a mirror and saying to himself how asinine he looked. Humour, after all, was a sign of decadence. No wonder the Japanese carried everything before them!

14   I was Headmaster of a Japanese School

My total stock-in-trade consisted of two Japanese words I had picked up many years before while travelling to Hong Kong on board a Japanese ship — *ano-ne* and *sodes-ka*. But I was no worse off than my fellows. We were as innocent of Japanese as babes unborn, when we assumed duty as teachers of Japanese.

I was posted to a phantom school. It had been used as an ammunition dump, and an explosion a few days after the Fall of Singapore had reduced it to a heap of rubble.

My first duty was to pay myself and my staff half-a-month's salary.

Our new salaries were calculated on the basis of our original salaries in accordance with a graduated scale. Thus men with $300 and over were given 45% of their original salaries. The percentage was higher for men who used to have less. Recipients of salaries of less than $100 got theirs in full.

The Singapore arrangement was unique. Elsewhere teachers were paid at a flat rate, regardless of qualifications, experience, length of service or category of schools. For we had three categories of schools — 'Former English

Schools', 'Malay Schools' and 'Chinese Schools'. Subsequently a fourth category was added — 'Indian Schools'. The arrangement worked in favour of 'Former English Schools'.

For this we had the Chief Inspector to thank. In antediluvian times he had been headmaster of an English school and in him we had a stubborn champion. He contended that as we were more highly qualified we deserved higher salaries. More highly qualified for what? This was the pertinent question of our colleagues in Malay and Chinese schools. For the teaching of English, of course. But we were all going to teach Japanese, and for this we were all starting from scratch.

But old E.V. Davies turned a deaf ear to all arguments, holding the breach single-handed against all comers and throughout the Occupation we teachers of Former English Schools were paid higher salaries.

E.V. was justified in us. For soon after, when concerts were got up for the greater glory of Nippon, our representatives played prominent parts in them, and the accruing credit went to buttress our claims to preferential treatment. Furthermore, our average mark was found to be the highest, when the results of the first Japanese examination were scrutinised.

This was contrary to expectation. For one would naturally have expected teachers of Chinese schools to shine, by reason of their command of *Kanji*, which was admittedly the worst snag in the path of the student of the Japanese language and which consists of Chinese characters masquerading as Japanese by being given a Japanese pronunciation. Thus we have a character which we pronounce *su*, meaning 'private' as opposed to 'public' which is *gung*. The Japanese pronounce it *watakushi* and it means 'I'. So for a man conversant with written Chinese, written Japanese holds no terrors. He can get the drift of a passage of written Japanese without knowing a single word of spoken Japanese.

Now, amongst us teachers of Former English Schools, the Chinese who could read Chinese could be counted on the fingers of one hand. And yet, handicapped as we were, we led on the stony road of mastery of the Japanese language. E.V. was justified in us. We were more proficient teachers of Japanese. When the curious-minded or malicious went on to ask why this was so, our answer came pat — we were more intelligent. That silenced the impertinent.

We were all dazed. For the firmament of heaven had cracked and jagged pieces had fallen on our heads. The huge gigantic fact that the Japanese were in our midst had taken all savour from life. Sleep didn't refresh nor food nourish. Laughter jarred. And the outlet of flippancy was denied us. We were thoroughly cowed. A cat might look at a king, but not we at a Nip. He might see in our eyes something he wouldn't relish.

So we stayed at home and forced our noses to the grindstone. We had to learn Japanese to keep ourselves alive. So we girded up our loins for an assault on *Nippon-go*. The Japanese gave us willing assistance. Japanese classes sprang up in every quarter of the town and suburbs, Japanese privates even giving up their spare time to teach us. Their enthusiasm for their own language was portentous. What was sauce for the goose was sauce for the gander. They tried to spread the knowledge of Japanese with an almost missionary zeal. One felt exasperated and yet impressed.

All Singapore made a rush for the new education. Some of us attended two, or even three schools a day.

Very little of this enthusiasm was inspired by genuine love for things Japanese. Most of it was the result of a love for novelty or was frankly utilitarian. A smattering of the language might come in useful when passing a barricade every half-a-mile. It might come in useful in our palavering with soldier visitors to our homes, a dose of Japanese seeming to go a long way to put them in good humour. And it might come in useful in our dealings with a generous soldier or officer who had a big say in the disposal of things after which we hankered.

For us teachers it was to be our means of livelihood. So we applied ourselves to it with varying degrees of success. Some were soon able to jabber in the new language, to the gratification of their Japanese visitors and to the chagrin of slower learners, who cursed them for setting them a pace with which they, the duller ones, could never hope to keep up.

At the start the highest class was Class V, corresponding to our pre-war Standard III. A time-table was hammered out by our inspectors and to this we adhered as closely as we could. The medium of instruction was perforce English.

Our hearts were not in our work. But to sit or stand and look at the children would invite comment from zealous parents and an inquisitive public, and might get ourselves and our inspectors into trouble. What a godsend our teachers of Physical Training and of Singing were! They and their work covered a multitude of sins. How could anyone accuse us of malingering, if the school hummed with activity?

In my school there were thirteen or fourteen of us to less than one hundred and fifty pupils!

For this we had a Nip to thank — Mr. Shinozaki, according to the testimony of our original Inspector of Former English Schools, a man who was in close contact with Mr. Shinozaki in Singapore and later on in Bahau, and who persisted in speaking well of Mr. Shinozaki in after days when speaking well of Nips was no longer in fashion.

The Japanese military had not been interested in schools. Children might loaf and teachers starve for all they cared. The re-opening of schools was not an item on their agenda.

But Mr. Shinozaki rushed here and there, trying to enlist the help of influential Japanese, and he eventually succeeded, so that permission was given to re-open Singapore schools.

Another difficulty arose. Parents were reluctant to send children to school. Schools were half empty. On his own authority Mr. Shinozaki lowered the minimum for a class to fourteen, thus giving jobs to thrice as many teachers as would have been possible if the pre-Occupation minimum had been adhered to.

One day Mr. Shinozaki said in confidence that he was less concerned about the teaching of Japanese than about the fate of teachers. His immediate problem was to give employment to as many of them as possible, he said, so that they might possess passes which would confer on them a measure of immunity from molestation.

The inspectors at the office had to justify their appointments to our Nip masters. That year saw a spate of circulars. Paper was plentiful. These circulars were a successful eyewash. Our inspectors thundered adjurations and warnings, holloing us on in the glorious march of all Asian peoples (notice we were no more 'Asiatics', we were 'Asians') in which we ourselves as teachers were playing glorious parts, eradicating all lingering traces of Anglo-American influences, inculcating the glorious spirit of Bushido (the way of the warrior). 'Bull-shit' came naturally to some of us. But we did not dare to utter the obscenity aloud. To play the wanton-wit at the expense of the majesty of Nippon was too perilous a proceeding. Perhaps our inspectors were not less irreverent in their heart of hearts, whatever serious faces they might pull in public. And I for one knew that my old friend E.V. had sufficient humour to smile wryly to himself while engaged in the concoction of hyperboles and olympian rumblings.

We owe a heavy debt of gratitude to E.V. and to the inspector of our own section. For they were efficient shock-absorbers, receiving the Japanese shocks and passing them on to us greatly reduced. My admiration for them steadily mounted as I watched their skilful gyrations on the tight-rope of their office and thanked my stars I was not in their shoes.

The way they used Physical Training was impressive. For what they called *Radio Taisho* they used sensibly planned series of simple exercises which could be done in unison to the rhythm of music sent over the radio. An increasing use was made of *Radio Taisho,* entailing the supply of radio sets to all schools. This was easy enough in those days, with so many confiscated and abandoned sets available.

I was an unwilling convert. It was only gradually that I came to realise what a potent instrument had been annexed by the Japanese educationists for the furtherance of the aim of enhancing nation-wide physical fitness. I came to have a mental picture of a people of one hundred millions springing out of bed early in the morning, sunshine or rain, summer or winter, tuning in to the broadcasting station and doing physical jerks to the rhythm of catchy tunes, and thoroughly enjoying the grind! It was an overwhelming thought and made me ashamed of myself and of my compatriots. Would we Chinese do it? It is too wild a thought to entertain for even a fraction of a second. It is enough to make a Chinaman sit on the floor and cackle with incredulous laughter.

But a doubt flits across my mind. What about those who have done the chore since childhood? Will the children in Chinese schools, for whom mass drill is part of the daily round, one day also prove fanatics for physical fitness, like the Japanese? And will the flag-waving that they have likewise learned from the Japanese one day turn them into chauvinists? That the native humour and indolence of our race will dilute and nullify the poison is a consummation devoutly to be desired.

The radio was used for another purpose, for developing a love for vocal music, and the success of the movement among the Japanese themselves was attested by the universal habit of singing among the soldiers. No one would say that the Japanese are a songful people like the Welsh. But singing had become a habit by a systematic cultivation in schools, providing an outlet for the emotions, directing them and thereby giving them intensity. This education of the emotions has never received due attention among us in Malaya, and I envied the Nips.

The songs themselves interested me and repelled me at one and the same time. They interested me because they gave me an inkling of the racial mind of the Japanese.

But there was one song that I was never tired of listening to. It had the authentic note of sincerity:

> "We go up to the mountains —
> We bleach among the mosses.
> We go down to the sea —
> We welter in the brine,
> But, whate'er betide,
> Rejoicing I die,
> For I die for thee."

It moved me to my depths, that simple song of self-dedication. I had not been so moved by any song since Armistice Day, 1917, when the schoolchildren of Singapore sang:

> "Land of our birth, we pledge to thee
> Our lives, our hopes, our years to be:
> When we are grown and take our place
> As men and women of our race."

That Japanese song made my heart ache thinking of the years in this land where all are for self and none for all, in which as individuals and as communities, we are grabbers, among people for whom 'disinterested' and 'uninterested' are synonyms.

I made the Japanese song the text of a talk at a School Assembly. A teacher, a woman and an old friend, was furious with me and took me to task afterwards. Was Saul also among the prophets? I was happy to find someone who had not given her heart away and proud to think that she had enough trust in me to speak so roundly.

For the dragon's teeth of distrust had been sown among us. Gone was mutual trust and confidence. We had learned to smile without sincerity. I was fortunate in that a third of my staff was made up of former pupils, and yet I did not feel safe! What injustices we all committed in our minds in those febrile days! And once I committed an act of injustice. I engineered the transfer of a teacher from fear of him, who, I am now sure, harboured no evil designs against me.

Once a serious complaint was lodged against one boy by a teacher. While I was investigating the matter, the boy ran home. The next day he returned armed with a letter from his guardian, in which he mentioned his connection with the *Kempeitai*.

In justice we must say that out of the three or four hundred teachers of the Former English Schools not one was actually betrayed by a colleague — surely a fact that redounds to the honour of our profession, and nine-tenths of us were passively pro-British, if not actually anti-Japanese.

In the retrospect one wonders whether our Japanese superiors had any suspicion of the truth. Were they, too, parties to the deception? Our Director of Education was a Capt. Ogawa, an Anglican and a gentleman. Our first Education Officer was Mr. Shinozaki. But he did not long remain with us. He soon went over to the Social Welfare Department. His successor was another captain, a man with a cherubic countenance whom we seldom saw. The third man was a tall lanky fellow with witch's teeth, who, a forbidding figure to the rest of us, was actually, according to those who saw him at closer range, a decent fellow. Once a young bounder kept pestering him with requests for more and yet more facilities for improving his command of *Nippon-go*, so as to render him more capable of serving Nippon. Putting a finger on his lips, Mr. Harada said "Yes"; putting the same finger on his heart, he said "No", and he wagged his head sagely.

It was only among the gate-crashers, men who were not in our ranks in pre-Occupation days, that a few genuine 'pro-Nips' could be found and even these were 'pro-selves', not 'pro-Nips', the success of Japan spelling success for themselves. Anyway, sycophancy on the Nips was a wonderful apprenticeship for life, and the arts thus learned and perfected would stand them in good stead in days to come.

We were provided with an unfailing stream of instructors. The classes, however, were so large that it was easy for anyone to malinger, if he or she wished to do so. But few of us did malinger. Most of us plunged into the waters of *Nippon-go* with considerable zest.

Our first instructor was a private named Kunitani. He knew some English and was perhaps a teacher of English by profession. One felt that he did his duty and no more. He was no fanatic, nor a hot-gospeller of hate, like Prof. Zimbo, who occasionally relieved him. This Prof. Zimbo obviously conceived himself a cut above poor Kunitani, to whom he administered a rebuke in public once. He was professor in the University of Tokyo, this Prof. Zimbo, and not a showman nor a strolling astrologist. He had the eyes of a tamer of wild beasts, however, full of malevolence and hinting at unguessed and limitless powers of compulsion. I looked at him and he looked at me. That one glance sufficed. Thereafter I schooled my eyes. Thereafter I was a man of the downcast glance. How he did hate us! And for no reason that I could see. We were amenable enough, subservient enough, thankful enough for every scrap he contemptuously tossed us. What a man! And yet what a calligraphist! He was the only Japanese I came across during the years of the Occupation whose Chinese calligraphy rose above the level of mediocrity. It was a joy, his calligraphy — at times I felt like squealing with delight as I watched his masterly production of strokes. How I wished I had stood in less fear of him! I would have gone up to him and asked him for a few specimens.

When a group of ex-Malayan Japanese returned from India, the duty of instructing us devolved on them. Among these were two women, Miss Misawa and Mrs. Sakai who had been for many years teachers in English Schools in Singapore. To their honour be it said that not once did they voice any hatred for the government they had once served. What was more, Mrs. Sakai seemed to have a soft spot in her heart for the English language. In our first *Nippon-go* examination there was a passage of Japanese for translation into English. Going over our results, Mrs. Sakai remarked wonderingly and with a touch of regret that we seemed to be forgetting our English. Replied a bright young thing: "But we thought you would want us to forget it!"

During the second year we had a chit of a girl for our instructor. She was a termagant! It was said that once, as a pupil of one of our schools, she had been rather unkindly treated by her teacher. If this was true, her attitude towards us, the older among the teachers of the Former English Schools, was comprehensible. How she revelled in humiliating us, in puncturing our pomposity and self-importance! Mercifully her sarcasms slipped harmlessly down our backs, as we didn't know enough Japanese to understand her.

The register was never marked by the instructor. It was marked by the monitor. The percentage of attendance was consistently high. Some of us would go to the class early, have ourselves marked present before the appearance of the instructor, and then disappear. Fortunately the register was never scrutinised by the instructor. But the possibility of scrutiny was always there. Once a teacher tried to improve on the existing arrangement. Meeting the monitor miles away from the school, he informed him that he did not intend going to the class, and would the monitor mind marking him present? If the instructor should ask any inconvenient question, the monitor could tell any lie that might occur to him. "What!" exclaimed the luckless monitor. "Tell a lie in Japanese, when I can't even tell the truth in it!" It came as a shock to one that glib lying in any language pre-supposes a tolerable command of the language in which one intends to lie!

There were we, sweating like galley-slaves, and to mighty little effect! One of us plastered the walls of his room with texts of Japanese words, which he was forever conning in a vain attempt to make them stick in the memory. It was *Nippon-go* the first thing in the morning and *Nippon-go* the last thing at night: ours were the labours of Sisyphus.

> "Let a man contend to the uttermost
> For his life's set prize, be it what it will!
> And the sin I impute to each frustrate ghost
> Is — the unlit lamp and the ungirt loin."

We were free from that sin. We did light our lamps and we did gird up our loins in pursuit of our life's set prize — a modicum of *Nippon-go* to pass muster, to enable us to feed ourselves and our families, and yet we remained frustrate ghosts.

So it is easy to imagine our exasperation at the sight of men covering the same ground with seven-league boots, men who seemed to be so pre-disposed to the Japanese language and who were so speedily habituated to it as to be able to rattle away in it in an unconscionably short time.

There was a meeting at which Japanese officers of high rank were present. We had been instructed to be present. There was speechifying on our part. It was an oratorical contest in Japanese. The Japanese present showed signs of approbation, nodding their heads. The nodding became brisk and vigorous when a speaker criticised the prevailing

97

methods of teaching Japanese and advocated the Direct
Method — and this in fluent Japanese. Luckily thoughts have
no power to kill. Else that man would have died on the
spot. He was recommending a few extra turns of the screw
in our torturing-machine, and we didn't love him for it!

> "The mountains look on Marathon
> And Marathon looks on the sea."

Would he force the reluctant sea to rise to the level of
Marathon? We didn't mind Marathon striving to rise to
the level of the mountains, but couldn't Marathon leave
us in peace, to ebb and flow at our own pace?

The Japanese headmaster of the Higher Normal School
paid my school a visit, to give it the look-over, to see
whether it was suitable as a training school for his young
men. When he found me the stuttering idiot that I was,
helplessly floundering in Japanese and answering him in
English, a gleam came into his eyes that boded me no good.

I had to get out. The close proximity of that man
would reduce me to a raving lunatic in a week.

For twenty-two months I had been the darling of the
Education Department, the people there conspiring to spoil
me. I had been posted to a school that was ten minutes'
walk of my house, a school hidden away in an inaccessible
spot six miles from town and half-a-mile from the main
road, and the lane leading to it was narrow and incon-
spicuous and in the worst state imaginable. They sent me
three or four former pupils as members of my staff, men
who knew my idiosyncracies and on whom I could lay all
the unpleasant burdens I would not dare to lay on others.
When the Inspector of Former English Schools was relin-
quishing his post to go to Bahau, it was agreed between
him and the Chief Inspector that I should be passed over,
on the ground that I was a bookworm and a dreamer, and
his successor, also a very good friend, did all he could to

ease my lot for me. The posting clerk — a former pupil — never failed to give me advance information on impending visits of inspectors or Japanese officials. Not that I had many visitors, for nine times out of ten, either they succumbed to the blandishments of schools on the way or, if they did arrive in the vicinity of my school, they got lost in the labyrinthine twistings and turnings of the lane.

How much luckier I was than S. for instance! He was headmaster of a school half-a-mile from the Education Office, fronting one of the busiest roads in Singapore, and so imposing and pretentious was the school building that it simply clamoured for attention, and attention it received from Japanese passers-by ranging from major-generals to privates, endless streams of them, and poor S. had to dance attendance upon them all.

But I never had a fraction of S.'s resilience and toughness. I felt I must get out or go mad. My friends, the Chief Inspector and Inspector of Former English Schools, rallied to my aid, helping me to concoct convincing reasons. They told the Japanese Education Officer that as my wife was suffering from consumption, it would be undesirable for me to remain. The Education Officer agreed, and I was allowed to resign. There was no red tape in my case, no delay. My letter was ante-dated by ten days and my release came in an hour from the time I had slipped into the office. So, after twenty-two months of headmastering a Japanese school, I joined the ranks of the unemployed.

Thus my fairy godmother saved me from the far greater vicissitudes that my colleagues were to experience subsequently. These came upon them after the appointment of a new Education Officer, a young man named Mori. This Mori was a veritable tyrant and sadist.

Mori was furious at finding so little progress in the mastery of *Nippon-go* among the teachers of Singapore in comparison with their compeers in his last post. He wanted to dismiss two hundred of them incontinently, and the inspectors were hard put to it to turn him from his purpose.

Mori sent out his fiat that teachers should be sent to assist in the 'Grow More Food' campaign. They were organised into twelve gangs. One gang dug from ten to one, a second from three to six. Thus the rotation was completed in six days. On Sundays four gangs dug at the same time.

This digging and planting was not the greatest hardship, however. How were they to get to the scene of the digging and planting? This was the greatest hardship. No transport was provided. Well and good if a man had a bicycle. The majority didn't.

A park four miles from town was chosen. The teachers suggested an alternative plan of having three places, so that a teacher could dig and plant at the place nearest to him or her. But Mori would have none of it. He had to have his pound of flesh.

Let us take the case of a man whose school was six miles away from town. He had a choice. He could come to town by tram or taxi and walk the four miles to the park, or alternatively, he could walk the whole of the ten miles. As accommodation in a tram or bus was almost impossible to get, and the fare for taxis prohibitive, the majority walked the whole distance. They dug for three hours and then walked ten more miles to get home. This regimen would have been excellent for healthy, well-fed men, but it was disastrous for the starvelings that most people in Singapore were at the time. One is not surprised that a few have died. One is surprised that so few have died.

He was no sentimentalist, that Mori of ours. He did not spare the women. He made them go through the same mill as the men. They too, had to go and dig. Go the women did, but the men would not allow them to dig except when the Japanese task-masters were present, which, mercifully, was not often. In return, some of the women, out of their meagre rations, gave the men some refreshment during the digging.

Among the gang-leaders was a young man from Kuala Lumpur who used to mark people present who were really absent. This deception of his was never discovered. If it had been, he would have received a few slaps and a kick or two, if nothing worse.

Hereafter let none say that teachers did not share the common lot. A few did indeed join themselves to the carrion-crows and batten on the public, blossoming out as princelings of the Black-marketing World, but, speaking as a whole, the teachers had too little enterprise and too many scruples, and in consequence shared the privations and tribulations of the generality.

I have before me a document entitled *Suggestions regarding the Improvement of Living Conditions for Teachers*, submitted by the 'Syonan Teachers' Association' and dated 25th April *Showa* 20 (i.e. 1945). The preamble runs as follows: "The economic condition of the average teacher has sunk very low ... So has his morale ... He cannot put his heart and soul into his work, such as the study of *Nippon-go*."

With suppliant tones they asked for an increase of rice ration of three katis a month. They asked to be allowed to make ropes for the military, in return for extra rations. They said that, as teachers, they needed foot-wear more than anyone else. They supplicated the Education Officer to take 'a personal interest' in them. "In all cases of accident and unforeseen troubles they beg him to help them." One hears an echo or two of the Litany. A pathetic phrase, that 'unforeseen trouble'. They were a thoroughly frightened lot, with pictures of the *Kempeitai* and their devilries occupying large spaces of their minds by day and by night.

There were the quondam magnificoes, the teachers of Singapore, once so resplendent in all their pomposity and self-satisfaction, now very bedraggled and very dejected, pleading piteously for a few crumbs from the Japanese table. How were the mighty fallen! "Good fellows, very good fellows; but vain, very vain."

15   Lim Bo Seng — II

Bo Seng left Singapore on Thursday, 12th February 1942 in a *sampan* and landed on a small Dutch island not far from Singapore. There he found a 30-ton steamer requisitioned by a party of British military and naval personnel who agreed to take Bo Seng and his comrades on board. That night the crew deserted. Bo Seng undertook to do the stoking and washing with the help of his party. They landed on the east coast of Sumatra and made their way to Padang on the west coast. There he was taken on board an Australian destroyer, from which he and his party as well as others were transferred to an Australian cruiser which arrived in Colombo on 5th March, having again and again stopped to pick up boatloads of escapees at sea.

From Colombo Bo Seng went to Bombay and from there he made his way to Darjeeling, where he succumbed to the magic of the mountains. He noted in his random jottings his dream of revisiting the place with his wife and children.

He was instructed to proceed to Chungking. There he was told to return to India and help to organise for war-service the many thousands of Chinese seamen stranded in Calcutta.

Also in Calcutta at that time was Lt. Col. Goodfellow, whom Bo Seng had met during his escape and who was now head of a group entrusted with the duty of establishing contact with the guerillas in Malaya. Goodfellow learned of Bo Seng's presence in Calcutta. A meeting was arranged at which were also present two men who were later to play leading roles as guerilla leaders in Malaya — Capt. Davis and Capt. Broome. The three men were at first inclined to fence with Bo Seng, but soon realised they were dealing with a man of an admirable directness. Bo Seng threw in his lot with theirs.

He returned to Chungking and got the consent of the Generalissimo. It was agreed that China should provide the men and Britain would arrange for the training and expenses of an organisation to engage in underground activities in Malaya. Bo Seng went round recruiting likely men and returned to India with a following of young men, mostly ex-Malayans eager to have another crack at the Nips. The 'training was carried on among the ruins of an "ancient Moghul fortress whose battlements frowned upon cliffs hundreds of feet sheer". He threw himself into this training with enthusiasm, but was never able to remain long with his men. He had to rush here and there, fighting the battles of preparation, torturing the unwilling dross to suit his purposes. He never suffered fools gladly, though he forced himself to suffer them patiently. Once he jotted in his diary: "This afternoon sleep was denied me. I pondered over my own behaviour during the journey up to the present. I can't help feeling that I have been too short-tempered with some of the members of my party." But a snapshot taken at the time shows a twinkling of the eyes and smiles playing round the lips which argue happiness found in congenial activity.

In May 1943, the first party left for Malaya, five men under the command of John Davis. They were carried into Malayan waters by a submarine and sent ashore in folding canvas boats. They landed at Pangkor, advanced a few miles inland and set up camp in the jungle. Fortune favoured them. They fell in with a patrol of guerillas. In November, after getting reinforcements, they went up the Perak River in a junk. Disembarking, they continued by night marches and eventually arrived at their destination, to find themselves among lean, wiry and tattered members of the main Resistance Army, who subsisted on meagre fare but had generous rations of songs and speeches, interminable speeches that would have turned delicate stomachs queasy but upon which simpler spirits throve exceedingly.

In December Broome led a party out of the jungle to get in touch with a submarine that was bringing more men and equipment. Finding the Japanese patrolling the area in force, they arranged to have two men keep the rendezvous at sea and they themselves returned to camp. One of the two men was Chin Peng, for nearly 30 years now the Secretary of the Malayan Communist Party.

Days passed and no news. But unknown to them, Chin Peng had successfully carried out his mission. His junk had been sighted by the submarine, which surfaced at nightfall and took Chin Peng and his companion on board. In the stuffy wardroom the two men conferred, Chin Peng and Bo Seng.

Bo Seng's instructions were to receive the reports of the guerilla leaders, give them advice and return in the submarine. But he had full authority to alter his plans, if he saw fit. He decided to join the guerillas.

All this happened unknown to his comrades in the jungle, into whose midst he walked with a grin on his face. His journey had not been uneventful. He had undergone examination by a Japanese soldier at one point and at another he had spent a night at a house not far from a place where a *suk-tsing* was going on, a cleaning-up which was so apt to end in a massacre.

The following is what Capt. Broome said: "It was thus that Lim Bo Seng joined us in our jungle camp. Within a few minutes of his arrival, he was deep in discussion of plans. Inactivity was torture to him. He must always be fighting, always pushing on towards the ultimate object. But in the jungle, when you are living in camp, there must perforce be many long dreary hours of inactivity, when there is literally nothing to do and a man has to search about and find his own means of keeping himself occupied. Bo Seng was not by nature an outdoor man, and though in his father's home in China he had seen plenty of old-fashioned country life, his real interests lay in the social contacts, the business problems and all the busy life of a big city. For such a man, the life of the jungle is a weariness and a strain. Nevertheless, he threw himself into the life of our camp with all his old energy, which we by then knew so well. He began to organise our commissariat. At that time, I am almost ashamed to say, we were living extremely well. All our food had to be brought up from the plains, but at that time we were living not far in, and the Japanese had not yet scented our presence in the area, so we were able to obtain all sorts of delicacies which we would have given our souls for later on. Bo Seng thought our cooking could be improved, so of course he set out to improve it himself. He claimed no knowledge of cookery but he was willing and anxious to experiment, and I must say his experiments were extremely successful. He took up his cooking as he took up everything else, determined to make a job of it, and in the short time he was with us, he made himself a first-class jungle cook. This was typical of the man. At one moment deep in plans of the highest importance, at the next bending over a cooking fire, and in each case, putting his whole soul into the work in hand."

Bo Seng always had the knack of concentrating all the powers of mind and body to a point, brushing aside all irrelevancies, clamping down the clamant thoughts and feelings that might weaken the flow of energy in the direction demanded by the needs of the moment.

After a conference at Resistance Army Headquarters, Bo Seng decided to go to Ipoh and himself direct the activities of the agents. His associates, while agreeing with him that his presence there would be invaluable, were yet apprehensive of the risks he would run, with his unmistakable characteristics, his gestures and foibles known to so many, owing to the extent of his business and other activities in pre-Occupation days. He was not a man people met and forgot. But he was set on going. He went to Ipoh, passing himself off as the uncle of the owner of the shop that was the hub of the organisation.

He made himself a prime favourite with some of the Japanese, using all the charm that indubitably was his, so that when he was arrested, seven of his Japanese friends, it was said, went to the *Kempeitai* to vouch for him and got a beating-up for their pains. He was arrested at the end of March 1944, and died in prison a few months after. He was 37 years old.

16 On Cads: by a Cad

There was a woeful falling off in morals, public and private.

We played the sycophants of Nips, not shamefacedly, but as men glorying in the successful pursuit of what deserves the approbation, and even the envy, of their fellows. We did not put our friendships under a bushel, we put them on a high hill, so that all might see and tremble.

Chan A and Chan B were heads of old and prominent Chinese families. According to Chinese notions of consanguinity, they were cousins.

Chan A was hard up. He wanted to dispose of a ring. He thought his nephew (the son of Chan B) might know of some prospective buyer. He entrusted the ring to the young man, who, after some time, returned and said that he had lost the ring. Would his uncle be satisfied with the payment of half the price of the ring? Chan A refused and went to Chan B to lodge a complaint. Chan B refused to accept responsibility, saying he had disowned his son.

Chan A was not satisfied. He wanted to start proceedings against his nephew. But he wisely saw a Japanese friend first. The Japanese assured him that as it was a civil case, he could safely proceed. So Chan A set the machinery of the law in motion.

But he had reckoned without his host. If he himself had wisely cultivated a Nip friend, so had his kinsman, whose friend was even more influential than his own, being a *Kempei* man.

Chan A was arrested and taken to the police station, where the preliminary investigation took place. This consisted of forty or fifty whackings with a 'wooden implement' laid on with right goodwill, so that it was soon broken. After that, he was taken to see his kinsman's Japanese friend, with whom Chan B and Chan B's son and daughter were in conference. The *Kempei* man told Chan A that the ring was worth only one-third the price he had asked for it. Would Chan A accept that sum? A kindly interpreter advised him to accept the offer, lest worse befall. This Chan A did, and was released.

The incident was symptomatic of a general coarsening of conscience. More and more we came to repudiate the claims men had on us: we refused to consider ourselves our brothers' keepers. It was each man for himself and the devil take the hindmost.

A famous American journalist on a visit to England during the war years remarked wonderingly and admiringly on the comparatively small part played by the Black Market in the life of the English nation — how it was generally considered un-English to try and beat the rationing system, which even the rich did not try to circumvent by using their superior purchasing power. According to him, this heartening phenomenon was due to the working of a sense of national solidarity that had not had its parallel since the days of Queen Elizabeth I.

Well, we in Malaya had no such solidarity. None had any scruples about patronizing the Black Market. Those of us who could afford the luxury hoarded foodstuffs, and if we saw men dying of starvation at our very door-steps, we merely shrugged our shoulders, pluming ourselves on our superior enterprise and foresight.

The sunning in public highways of rice that had gone green from long storage was surely an insult to the starving and would have caused a riot had we had any of the solidarity that so impressed the American visitor to England.

We are all familiar with the usual battery of arguments against primitive communism — that even if all the necessaries were pooled and shared out, the lot of the poor would not be appreciably improved. But reasonably or unreasonably, many of us felt that had there been greater willingness to share the common lot, the Black Market would not have played the havoc that it did. If the rich did not hoard so frantically, the rat population would have benefitted less and the human population more: the not-so-rich would have had a chance of getting something.

Hatred was generated in the hearts of many of us, not against the Nips only, but also against our own people: against the shareholders of the 'Black Marketeers, Unlimited' who were battening on the miseries of others, against the jackals who were so fertile of ingenious suggestions for new *kumiais* and who caroused so callously and so cynically in amusement parks while the rest starved.

The police got a large share of the hatred. In the first place, the police had shown themselves apt pupils of the Nips, delighting in cruelty.

Next, they did not share the common lot. Policemen touring the markets and helping themselves to fish and meat was no uncommon sight.

As for the higher ranks, they were living on the fat of the land. Their needs were never forgotten by the keepers of markets.

A police inspector in Singapore, a favourite of the Nips, went to a hospital to give his doctor a present of bread, white wheaten bread, in 1943, a year and a half after the rest of the population had seen the last of it. According to him, he had a daily supply of the bread and there was enough for him to give some away.

A police inspector in Malacca regularly sent his servant to the market to wait for the fish-cars. Whichever fish-car arrived first had the honour of a visit from this man. A large fish or two would go into his basket and he would trot home. Not a word was said.

A veterinary surgeon in the same town once did the same. He sent his servant. The reception this man had was instructive. He was sent away empty-handed. There was no reason whatsoever why a fish-dealer should show courtesies to a veterinary surgeon.

Another police inspector was in charge of imports. Every time a *tongkang* arrived with foodstuffs, he was sure to have his share put aside for him and, if the dealers could be believed, the tariff he had drawn up was far from modest. These, however, were mere peccadilloes. If a Black Marketeer was making his tens of thousands, why should the police have scruples about relieving him of a thousand or two? After all, he was beholden to them for their complaisance: they could so easily have placed difficulties in his way. And why should they not accept a secondary income from the owners of the eight hundred gambling-dens in Singapore in return for kindly closing their eyes to what was going on? After all, they were ordinary people and had to live.

The rest of the population envied them their opportunities. Given the same chances, everyone would have done what they did.

The real cause of the hatred lay elsewhere. It lay in the active and willing participation of the police as a body in the Japanese enormities. For instance, one cannot but feel that the Malay inspector who laid on his blows with a leather belt day after day on a Malay suspect until his victim died was a free agent, and not only a man carrying out orders. Nor can we conscientiously say that this was an exception. It was the rule, not the exception, as it were the portion of an iceberg that is visible.

Let us take the hypothetical case of a Black Marketeer. He was milked by informer after informer. Eventually he failed to satisfy one informer. This man engineered a raid on his premises. Sugar was found. He was taken into custody. A *Keibuho* (Probationary Police Inspector) was entrusted with the investigation. This man had power to do anything he might think fit. The suspect's family came forward with money, and the *Keibuho* was induced to exercise moderation. In due course a clean bill was returned and the man was discharged, say, in a month or six weeks, none the worse for his stay in the police station. But if no such inducement was forthcoming, the *Keibuho* proceeded in another fashion. He put the suspect through a gruelling interrogation day after day, varied with blows, slaps and kicks. To make him more amenable to reason, burning cigarettes would be used to start with. Next would come applications of the 'water-treatment' and the 'electric treatment', until the victim caved in and agreed to sign an 'I.P.' (Investigation Paper) in which he confessed to the alleged offence.

The 'I.P.' was held to be sufficient evidence and on the strength of it the accused had sentence passed on him.

And this was not the sum total of the mischief the police were capable of doing in this one case. For the accused had, in the course of interrogation, divulged the identities of all who had had dealings with him and all these were possible recipients of the attentions of the police and possible cows for them to milk.

It is as easy to get up a rage (even a righteous rage) as it is to get up a thirst. But, placed in the same circumstances, are there many of us who would have behaved differently? The system was to blame, not the individuals caught in it. For there were no checks on the power of the police — no Penal Code, no Law of Criminal Procedure, no Police Regulations, to which they were answerable. They had absolute power, and absolute power had corrupted absolutely.

One wonders whether the police in Singapore ever had any illusions regarding their own popularity with the population. The police in the small stations in the countryside had none. They vanished overnight the moment the Japanese surrender was known. A vigorous man-hunt started, the informers being the quarries this time. Among those who were smoked out, a few were given a dose or two of the medicine they had so often caused to be given to others, and it was surprising how little they seemed to relish it.

A young Seremban informer made for home as fast as his motor-cycle could carry him. He was waylaid and shot dead on the outskirts of his hometown. His mother, a widow, was living in a ramshackle hut in a small fishing village, to which the young man used to pay visits and where he was a general favourite. Never once had he put a neighbour into trouble. His death came as a shock to everyone in the village. It is easy enough to consign a class to the devil, but when that class resolves itself into individuals, one does not find sitting in judgment so easy.

Her only son dead, that widow was promptly. robbed of all the money she had — sixteen hundred dollars in 'Tiger' notes (Straits Settlements currency) hidden in a pillow. The son had eaten sour grapes and the mother's teeth were set on edge.

Where power is, there is always possibility of abuse of that power, even under the most favourable conditions. Human nature being what it is, public servants are only too prone to forget that they are servants of the public and come to consider themselves as conferring favours when they are merely doing their duty.

If this is so in normal times, when there are checks and counter-checks, how much worse it must have been during Japanese times, when these checks were no longer operative, when opportunities were increased a hundredfold, and when a man's salary hardly sufficed for two days' marketing.

These opportunities varied enormously in scope and frequency. Some departments could facilitate or obstruct to such good effect that they became veritable gold-mines for their personnel.

The Japanese heads of departments must have known what was going on. Many of them must have sympathised with their subordinates. One head of department was said to have issued verbal instructions deprecating hurry in the transaction of business: his subordinates should use due care and discretion and be sure to satisfy themselves first. The rambling phraseology gave a sufficient hint of his kindly intentions, and they did not fail to act up to them.

Strange though it may seem, this widespread venality did not occasion any · bitterness in the victims. They grumbled, indeed, now and then, but on the whole, there was surprisingly little venom. There was a measure of fellow-feeling for those who were mulcting them, and they dished up the gratification (illegal indeed, but customary) with a touch of friendly condescension, and with a shrug of the shoulders, saying in effect "Ah, the poor devils, too, must live."

This realistic spirit was equally evident in people who had occasion to go to the government hospitals. Gifts were given and taken with the utmost naturalness. The labourer was worthy of his hire. For no sensible person could imagine that the salaries of doctors, nurses and attendants represented just hire; and so services which in normal times are rendered in the ordinary course of duty, and for which the renderer is held to have been sufficiently remunerated out of public funds, came to partake of the nature of personal favours, for which due appreciation was called for.

The practice played havoc with professional dignity. Many a doctor must have blushed when first given a basket of eggs, or a couple of fowls, or a 'red-packet', but want gives short shrift to false shame.

The descent was correspondingly easier for nurses, dressers and attendants, whose inner resistances were easier to overcome.

The rot once started, what assurance was there that it would not spread? We all love a generous giver and hate a niggardly one. Thus the rich patients were fussed over and the indigent neglected, sometimes even bullied.

My first impulse is to dump the Black Marketeers in medical supplies among the villains of the Occupation. If ever money was tainted, theirs was. Collectively they were responsible for many deaths, not directly, of course, but indirectly, through denial of supplies.

And yet it is difficult to see what else they could have done. For many of them, the purveying of medicine had been a life-long occupation, and if they had allowed themselves to be moved overmuch by foolish scruples, they and theirs would have starved. Let us suppose some of them had been too squeamish to continue. Let us suppose these released all their supplies cheaply. What would have happened? The supplies would not have gone directly to those who needed them so desperately. They would have been snapped up by dealers less harassed by their consciences. The quixotic dealers would have injured themselves and would not have benefitted the sufferers.

Thus these men were as much the victims of circumstances as those who were their victims.

That a few of these men did not feel wholly comfortable in their minds at the start is sufficiently shown by the rationalisation in which one of them indulged. "If I don't make the money, someone else will. I look on the money as a gift from God, and I shall share it with the needy."

A man knelt on both knees before his millionaire doctor and placed palm against palm in supplication. The doctor spurned him as one would spurn a mangy dog rubbing against one's leg.

To the same doctor went a man who was a worm and not a man, to beg for some calcium sandoz for his consumptive wife. He thought the doctor might remember the kindnesses he had received in the days of his orphanhood from the consumptive's father. He was given half-a-dozen ampoules and told not to come again. What his wife needed, he was told, was not calcium sandoz, but exercise and nourishing food.

17   Exultations and Agonies

The dun days of the Japanese Occupation were an ideal season for rumination, for chewing the cud of fancies pleasant and unpleasant.

In 1912, in a short-lived bookshop in Penang, a lad of thirteen, an orphan and a charity-boy, flotsam and jetsam washed by the waves of circumstance on Malayan shores, his share of the household chores done, helped to keep shop. They were hours of unalloyed delight. He was no longer a household drudge. Customers were few and far between. He could give himself up to the *Books for the Bairns*, of which there were stacks and stacks. He was, for the nonce, of the company of the gentle-born and highly-bred, his lowly state forgotten.

To that delectable world the rudiments of English he had picked up in the course of his three years' schooling were the 'Open Sesame', the key that unlocked to him secrets that would give a meaning to life and render it tolerable.

This, I think, was not an experience peculiar to that lad. It must have been the common experience of many lads similarly circumstanced, for whom England was a kindly foster-mother, who, if they owed their physical existences to China or India, yet owed all their mental and spiritual development to England. To these England gave not her 'ways to roam' but she gave them the freedom of the manor of her quintessential self — her literature. For that high courtesy they could never be sufficiently thankful.

Do a Chinaman a kindness. He does not say "Thank you". But he remembers you. He considers ingratitude one of the mortal sins. One of his deepest convictions is that if a debt is not paid in this incarnation, it will have to be paid in a future one.

Thus for many in this land, the ideas and ideals with which they confronted life were those given by England. Men might point the finger of scorn at them. They were denationalised, monstrosities, loathsome hybrids, leprous, and should hide their heads in shame. But, somehow, they were unrepentant. They were foundlings, they agreed, but they were ashamed neither of their fostering nor of their foster-mother.

One man, giving evidence at a war trial, was asked by the counsel for the defence whether he knew of any anti-Japanese elements in Singapore. He said he did. Would he say who these were? "All Singapore" was the dramatic reply. It was true. Except for a tiny section made up of the beneficiaries of the Japanese regime, all Singapore was anti-Japanese. To say, however, that only those who had received an English education were anti-Japanese would be to lie. But to say that those who had received an English education were as staunch as any other category of men would be a sober statement of fact, and an understatement.

That Penang bookshop had an Englishman for a customer one day. Anxious to please, the lad fluttered round him, 'sirring' him assiduously. The customer, about to depart, admonished the lad, warning him against sycophancy, telling him that an Englishman's gorge would rise at the sight of grovelling.

In 1919 the pupils of a Singapore school were going in a procession to the Victoria Memorial Hall for the annual prize-giving. As they were crossing High Street, a European in a rickshaw insisted on crashing his way across the procession. A young teacher laid hands on the rickshaw and forced it back. The European got down to teach him a lesson. Two other Europeans intervened. Their intervention might have been inspired by a desire to save a heaven-born from the ridicule of a street fracas, but it might equally have been inspired by disapprobation of the unmannerly crasher. If so, it was an expression of the Englishman's love of fair-play, and it was as such an expression that it remained in the mind of that teacher, whom his hefty opponent could have pulverised by a couple of blows.

An Asiatic motorist charged with a traffic offence was tempted to plead guilty, pay the small fine and have done with the whole business. But he defended himself, apologising to the magistrate for taking up so much of the court's time. The magistrate assured him that he was right in defending himself.

It was the amalgam formed by experiences of this kind that constituted the touchstone by which we in Malaya tested the professions and behaviour of our Nip masters and found them far to seek. The Pax Japonica, we realised, was far inferior to the Pax Britannica we had known in the days of plenitude and peace.

We Chinese are obsessed by a painful sense of the instability of life, of the fickleness of fortune. The gods are envious of human felicity. "If a man has blessings, let him not enjoy all; if he has power, let him not use all" expresses this sense of man's insecurity in the world. This sense may give poignancy to our sojourn on earth; it may be the stuff of poetry. But, perverse men that we are, we long for firm ground beneath our feet so that we can stride along confidently and unafraid.

To British law we in Malaya had owed the inestimable blessing of having some firm ground in the quagmire of life. If we did this or this, we rendered ourselves liable to the pains and penalties of the law; if we did not, we were safe. Within the confines of the law, therefore, the incalculable did not play so devastatingly with our peace of mind.

The Japanese did away with all that. As one shopkeeper put it, one's head might be on one's shoulders in the morning and by the evening the two might have parted company.

Three thousand years ago, King Wu of the Chow dynasty ranged through feudal China, suppressing the turbulent barons of the empire. The cry of the common people was not against his carrying war into their lands; it was against his slowness in coming. This cry was echoed and re-echoed by the people of Malaya during the Occupation. Again and again we mistook thunder for the roar of guns, so foolish we were! The cry of anguish of every heart was "How much longer? Why are the British so slow?" When bombs at long last began to fall in Singapore, men didn't dive into the nearest drains. They clambered up trees. The dominant feelings were not fear and anxiety. They were exhilaration and exultation.

The Tyrant of Yin, pointing to the sun, exulted: "I shall remain King as long as that sun remains in the sky." The common people, victims of his misrule, cocking an eye at the sun said: "Ah, Sun, when will you perish? If you would only perish, we won't even mind perishing with you!" These words exactly expressed the feelings of the people of Malaya, too. We had no illusions. And there were Japanese who said to their hosts, over their cups, "We know we shall have to die. But don't you think you'll live. We'll see that you die with us."

To the Chinese the Japanese iterated the claim that their rule exemplified the 'Way of the King' and not the 'Way of the Overlord'.

These contrasted terms have been familiar to the Chinese for the last two thousand years. The 'Way of the King' has stood for the government of the people for the people, and the 'Way of the Overlord' the government of the people for the ruler. The first has been characterised by justice and peace, the second by war and rapine.

Paradoxically enough, the most peace-loving nation in the world has had the most sanguinary history of all. The history of China is a history of the martyrdom of man and, reading it, one involuntarily shrinks away from that pestilential race of vermin, and one wonders how it has been allowed to crawl on the face of the earth for so long.

But the heart of the race has always been right. It has hungered for righteousness. The conviction that government should be based on justice and mercy, not on fear or force — this conviction has become a part of the racial consciousness. All have it, young and old, learned and unlettered. They go one step further. They imagine that the universe is founded on morality — a wholly unwarranted assumption. The most poignant expression I know of was that given by a woman whose husband was among those butchered. Loosening her long hair, she offered sacrifices to the spirits, calling on them to avenge her wrongs, and finished up by flinging a challenge full in the face of the Creator. "If you allow such things to go on," she stormily said, "you must be a blind old dodderer!"

I heard the words *Jippun mo goo* (Japan no long) from the lips of ignorant men, hardly able to scrawl their names. Whence came this adamantine conviction of theirs? It issued from the subterranean idea of the essential morality of the universe. Look at Japanese things, they said, at their toys and bicycle-tyres. Nothing that the Japs made could last. Neither would they last.

In W.H. Hudson's *Hampshire Days*, there is an unforgettable account of the instinctive reactions of the parasitical young cuckoo to the pressure of its foster-brothers, inducing in him paroxysms similar to those in an epileptic. It shrinks as though pricked by hot needles. It struggles madly to get rid of the offending objects.

This passage mirrored my state of mind during the Occupation. The proximity of the Nip induced in me a feeling of intolerable irritation, of mounting exasperation.

I did not hate the Nip. On the contrary, I admired him in one particular; he knew how to die and I had my doubts whether I would, if it came to the pinch. We had many things in common, the Japanese and we, a weakness for slippers, for instance, and willingness to serve a friend, cost what may. When they splashed the Chinese newspapers with the slogan 'Same race, same culture', I could not but yield a qualified though unwilling assent. But somehow they and their ways got on my nerves. They wore their rue with a maddening difference.

It was fortunate for me that during the last eighteen months I was at the seaside, nine miles from a small town, so that I did not see a single Nip for days on end.

An anecdote from *The Four Books* often came to my mind in those days. A disciple asked Confucius about the spirits. "Respect them and give them a wide berth" was the quick reply, the ordinarily so serious Confucius relaxing for once, pleased with his own wit, perhaps. Yes, it was sage advice. Respect the Nips — and give them a wide, wide berth.

I was not the only practitioner of that policy apparently. Seven months after the surrender of Japan a European doctor, an ex-internee, giving evidence at the trial of a war criminal said he had never seen the accused. He had always avoided meeting the man. "Nor, for the matter of that," he added, "did I see any other Japanese in camp. I took care to keep away from them. I don't like them. I hate their smell." That amiable doctor was deliciously frank. But I could not claim the merit of hating the Nip. Nor could I say that I ever found the smell of that animal particularly offensive, which, I suppose, was due to the fact that we were varieties of the same species. Nevertheless, I agree with the sage doctor that the safest course, under the circumstances, was to give the Nips a wide, wide berth.

There were times, however, when I felt that I could forgive the Japanese a great deal if they had only shown a wee bit of humour, if they could only smile at their own posturings, if they showed any sign of realising the ludicrous discrepancy between their pretensions and their actual performance — the mountain making so great a fuss to bring forth so small a mouse.

And they would vomit so many uncouth expressions in their asinine *Syonan Shimbun* to which we were reduced for our scraps of news!

Our own behaviour during the early months of the Occupation reminded me irresistibly of piglings stumbling over each other in their eagerness to get at the maternal paps. Whoever succeeded in getting in a suck at a Nip was rewarded with a 'protection paper' and was the envy of all his neighbours. Protection against what, or from whom? Common logic says 'protect someone from someone else'. From whom, in this case? From the English and Americans? They were safely cooped up in Changi. From evil-doers among ourselves? They were cowed by the quick and summary justice meted out by Nippon. Then protection from whom? Common logic, however, was too mundane for the children of the Moon Goddess, and I wondered if any of the fortunate recipients ever pulled wry mouths.

Two men were stopped at the Johore Causeway and questioned as to their destination. "Singapore," said one. He was allowed to proceed. "Syonan," said the other, anxious to air his knowledge of *Nippon-go* and to please the sentry. Please the sentry he did. The Jap grunted approvingly. But the man who had said "Singapore" was pulled back and manhandled.

The Nip was as inscrutable as fate and as incalculable as a thunderclap. And yet he was surprised that he was not a great success in the winning of hearts.

18   Sayonara

"How long, O Lord, how long" was wrung out of us countless times during the Occupation.

In his *Ballad of the White Horse* Chesterton makes King Alfred say "If that which is forever is, or if our hearts will faint with bliss, seeing the stranger go."

How we longed to see the stranger go! At the very thought of his going, our spirits would faint with the bliss of anticipation. That he would one day go, we were sure of. But could we last out the period of waiting? The end of our resources was in sight; the end of the Nip regime was not.

The chances of our survival were slender enough. We made a shrewd guess at the ultimate purpose of the tunnels honeycombing the island. They might one day serve as catacombs for us.

We were urged to evacuate to spots less dangerous and more favoured in the way of food, to return to the land, to dig and delve, to grow our own food. A slogan was coined and diligently circulated, consisting of four Chinese characters which went trippingly on the tongue, to the effect that manual labour was holy. The newspapers treated us to dissertations on a rational economy for Malaya. The iniquitous British, they told us, had always sacrificed

Malaya's interests on the altar of imperialism, forcing us to produce rubber rather than food, not caring a brass farthing whether we ate or starved in a crisis, whereas the Japanese, in their paternal solicitude for us, were moving heaven and earth to procure food for us. If we had something to eat, we should bless Nippon, and if we starved, we should curse Britain.

Few were aware of the food policy of the British Government during the months preceding the Japanese invasion, how it had stretched Malaya's financial resources to the uttermost to lay in sufficient quantities of food to last us two or three years. So the insidious Nip propaganda would have succeeded with a section of our population, had there been no mental resistances to overcome. But we hated the Nips too much to believe any good of them, and besides, their propaganda was very clumsy. "The lady doth protest too much."

We were unjust to some Nips, to Shinozaki for instance, who, we now see, was genuinely interested in the success of the two colonies he had sponsored — Bahau for the Eurasians and Endau for the Chinese. But we were unconvinced and very suspicious. What assurance had we that these colonies were real sanctuaries and not concentration camps for irreconcilable elements, of which the Japs could make a holocaust at the giving of a pre-arranged signal?

The end was drawing near. Our quislings were progressively drawing in their horns, paying court to one-time victims.

The newspapers came out with a report of the bombing of Hiroshima with a bomb of a hitherto unknown type. The damage was negligible, however, they said. Two days later came an admission of thousands of casualties. But in the interval there had been an unprecedented crop of rumours, to which we lent greedy ears. The effects had been cataclysmic, we were told. Japan's will-to-war had been pulverised. She was suing for peace.

The news seemed too good to be true. A cold fear gripped our hearts. Could it be that the rumours emanated from the *Kempeitai* and were disseminated by their underlings to tempt disaffection to rear its head, so as to facilitate a *Kempei* harvesting of heads?

No, we were not going to throw caution to the winds. We who had managed to keep our heads on our shoulders for three and a half years were not going to risk them now. So we walked circumspectly in those days, forcing ourselves to preserve equable exteriors, when all the while we were a maelstrom within, our hearts pounding away at the thought of approaching deliverance, our legs going soft with exquisite anticipations.

Unobtrusively we studied the countenances of our Nip masters — masters who would be no masters in a short while, if rumour did not lie. What we saw gave us hope. For we saw signs of great mental strain, suggesting sleepless nights and foodless days. There were constant comings and goings, confabulations lasting for hours, punctuated by loud guffaws got up for our benefit. Our hopes mounted.

At last the Nips steeled themselves for a public announcement. This was made by Mr. Shinozaki at a large gathering at which the guests had plenty to eat and plenty to drink, even beer. Mr. Shinozaki broke down.

The next day, at the Municipal Building, there was a gathering of the Japanese staff, at which the *Kimigayo* was sung for the last time in our hearing — that dirge of a Japanese national anthem, and on this occasion we were not deaf to its dignity and pathos.

On the same day the announcement was repeated in the newspapers, which cheapened the tragedy of a great fall, however, by their mouthings about humanity, which raised the gorge in those who could not forget the butchering of three and a half years before.

There was not a word about surrender. Stripped of verbiage, the announcement amounted to this: "His Imperial

Majesty, to save Asia from Anglo-American domination, declared war in December 1941. Now, in August 1945, graciously taking cognizance of the readiness of the British and Americans for peace, and wishing to save mankind from more slaughter and devastation, His Imperial Majesty has been pleased to declare peace." Thus the Son of the Moon Goddess and Vicegerent of God on earth made peace as he had made war — by his simple fiat. He said "Let there be peace", and there was peace. His godhead had suffered no eclipse, his majesty no diminution. On the contrary, he had received an accession of majesty. For not only the Japanese, his own people, but all the peoples of the world had been covered by his mantle and owed him eternal gratitude for the inestimable blessing of peace.

That tremendous leap into the empyrean of high falutin' left us gasping, robbed of our just triumph. For the Nip was unvanquished. He had not surrendered. He had merely obeyed his man-god. He could hold his head high, transfigured into a veritable paladin by his precious gift for rodomontade and self-deception. The Japanese sun had never shone with such effulgence on its noon-day as it did at its setting. Cold fear gripped our hearts. What assurance had we that it would not one day rise again and shed its baleful beams upon men?

That women who had found Nip charms irresistible should voice unqualified confidence in the ultimate return of the Nip was not surprising. The wish was father to the thought. But what reason had the inhabitants of a small fishing-village to share that confidence, that hope? The Nips had given them little beyond benevolent professions and ardent protestations of everlasting love.

We shall never know how many suicides there were. Some favoured the traditional *hara-kiri*, scooping out entrails in the high Japanese fashion. Others preferred lone revolver-shots, and yet others group-suicides, one party blowing up their house and themselves holding high revels in it. For whichever way they adopted, boisterous junketing seemed the invariable prelude.

The vast majority decided to live, of course. They first made provision for the temporary wives and the children. Few women were a fraction as lucky as that Eurasian woman in Java who was invited by her paramour to help herself to as much as she fancied from a hoard worth four hundred million dollars. The majority had only the reversion of the furniture which they had to remove speedily.

What a change there was in our Nip masters in those days! We beheld them sloughing their arrogance. The Nip is nothing if not thorough. If he has to eat humble-pie, he eats it with such a grace as to make even his worst enemy relent. Once again we remembered the courteous Nip shop-keepers of Middle Road of pre-war days who used to bow a customer in and bow him out again with equal affability, even if he had bought nothing.

How generous they were! They sowed gifts among men. And among women. There was no dearth of recipients.

They entertained themselves and their local friends lavishly. The board groaned with the load of viands. The starvelings looked on with envy, consoling themselves with the thought of approaching retribution on Nip satellites. Poor deluded fools! Little did they realise how wide of the mark they were.

We were outwardly subdued but inwardly effervescing. We were scrupulously courteous to our Nip masters at the office, especially at closing time, anxious to give our due tribute of *sayonara* to every mother's son of them. To our chagrin there were few to receive it. They had slipped away before time.

An Indian schoolmaster invited four friends to dine and wine. They expected some local brew. But they saw two bottles of Australian beer and a tin of English cigarettes to which their host had held on for three and a half years in the stubborn expectation of the event. The beer was somewhat flat for long keeping, but they were duly sensible of the honour their host was doing them and were overcome by wonder at his preternatural strength of purpose.

The junketing was universal, though on a modest scale in most households, by reason of narrowness of means. Everyone felt that the occasion could not be allowed to pass by without celebration, though few dared to do it too openly.

One party had their fling in a restaurant. Into their midst came two *Kempei* men, who, after a long grim look, contented themselves with a *"Makan besar, ka?"* (a big feed, eh?). An intrepid diner volunteered the information that the feasting was on the occasion of the birthday of one of the party. The *Kempei* men, after another grim look, went away. The diners incontinently fled, dinner unfinished.

A Eurasian family hung out the Union Jack and the Stars and Stripes on 21st August, rejoicing the eyes of the passers-by. Not of all passers-by, though, not of the Nips, who went louring, glowering by. That night a Nip came into their compound. The family kept their doors stubbornly shut, and after the Nip had gone away, they went to a neighbour's house and spent the night there, returning the next morning.

At the end of August, Malacca was gay with flags, among them an enormous Union Jack that had been hidden for three and a half years in the vestry of the Anglican church by a consumptive-looking Chinese priest whom one would have thought the last person to commit such an indiscretion.

The *Kempeitai* condescended to plead with the Chinese leaders, asking them to have some regard for Japanese 'face', begging them to postpone the tomfoolery until the British had taken over.

The financial and commercial barometer of the town rose rapidly. There was a rush to unload 'banana' notes, that is, Japanese military scrip, in exchange for 'Straits Settlements' notes, or for goods. Everything was acceptable; anything anyone offered for sale was snapped up eagerly. Prices soared. 'Straits Settlements' notes rose from 12:1 to 30:1. The price of gold rose in proportion, its peak at $110,000 a tahil.

The Japanese took a hand in the game. They offered all their stocks, military and civilian, for sale at prices far below those prevailing. A mad rush followed. Enterprising men formed syndicates to buy these goods. The Japanese ostentatiously burned the notes, buttressing the belief that their military scrip would eventually have a value. As their hoards of Nip notes grew smaller and smaller, operators began releasing their 'Straits Settlements' notes and their gold, the value of which sagged. When this happened, the Japanese began buying through their jackals, and so unobtrusively and efficiently was this done that by the time the operators realised what was happening, the Nips had laid in considerable amounts of 'Straits Settlements' notes and of gold.

Fortunes were made and lost. Among the heavy losers, some committed suicide, lacking philosophy to return to the gutters from which so many of them had originally come. Whenever we heard of the death of one of the more notorious among Nip jackals, we experienced elation rather than pity, and our regret was that there were so few of these suicides, knowing that most of them would live to enjoy their loot for many a long day, honoured citizens.

At length streams of lorries headed for Jurong, packed with household furniture, bedding, refrigerators, carpets.

Rumour said that the Japs were collecting the materials for a grand bonfire. If they were not to enjoy these things, the British should not enjoy them either. But we soon realised that we had misread the Nips. They had been instructed to concentrate at Jurong, and were thus wisely providing for themselves the means of a pleasant stay there. We remembered the lugubrious procession of three and a half years before, when our internees had to march the whole way, first to Katong, then to Changi, staggering under the loads they had to carry.

All these days we had been a very well-behaved lot, dazed with happiness or absorbed in commerce. Now we realised the rapid suction of Nips from our midst. All, or nearly all the offices were emptied of Japanese. Only a few buildings were guarded by sentries. We lost no time. We looted every empty building, every vacant house on the principle that whatever was unclaimed and untenanted was Jap property and fair game. At one place we stripped a house of doors and windows, rafters and tiles.

Some of us count ourselves fortunate in that we witnessed a scene of retribution, modest indeed, but manna to the unenterprising and self-righteous beholder. A satellite had been bequeathed furniture by his Nip principal which he loaded into rickshaws and was carrying away, when he was surrounded by a crowd of guttersnipes, some of whom hurled insults at him while others plucked the stuff from his rickshaws and threw them on the road to be retrieved and carted away by willing hands.

Now was the time for paying off old scores. Tram-cars were stopped and the drivers and conductors assaulted. We could not find it in our hearts to condemn this wild justice, long overdue, which we were too squeamish to mete out ourselves. Indeed, we were thankful to our guttersnipes for doing it for us.

Sikh watchmen and Malay policemen had made themselves scarce. A few were dug out and given a bit of what they deserved.

Both the looting and assaulting were done mainly by boys. A few grown-ups directed operations, pedalling their push-bikes and blowing their whistles.

Of course, there were miscarriages of justice. And there must have been many cases of private revenge. Some men had severer trouncings than they deserved, but among those who deserved summary justice many got off without a scratch, having squared the underground leaders, purchasing amnesty. Among these children of darkness who were wiser than the children of light were Formosans who simply faded out, thanks to the assistance of friends. For them the fading out was easy enough. They look Chinese and they speak Chinese. They did not even have to change their names. They only had to change the pronunciation of their names. A Hayashi Shiroyama for instance, could in a trice transform himself into a Lim Peh San and melt away.

On the morning of 4th September, we were reminded of a vivid Chinese expression about the sprouting of bamboo-shoots after a spring shower. For lorry after lorry appeared, each with slogans, each packed with gesticulating, vociferating humanity. They were the representatives of a host of political organisations ranging from the most awesome red to a pale, innocuous pink.

On 5th September at 3.30 p.m., British warships were first sighted.

The troops landed, prepared for all eventualities. The re-occupation proceeded without a hitch. The welcome the crowds gave them was as sincere as it was hearty. It was the very opposite of the frigid reception we had given the Nips three and a half years before.

For days afterwards, whenever a white man appeared in Chinatown, he was sure to be surrounded by Chinese boys, and their obvious pleasure at the sight of him must have embarrassed many a shy man, they tumbling over each other in their eagerness to touch him, hailing him as 'Joe' and, irreverent as ever, referring to him among themselves as 'Red-haired Devil', but in affection, as it were pronouncing a pet-name caressingly, and he grinning like a veritable jackass, vainly striving to express goodwill and fellow-feeling, neither conversant with the other's lingo. Their welcome was spontaneous and generous without a touch of mercenariness. Nothing could have been further from their minds than the capitalising of friendship. The cadging and the pestering came afterwards, when the ecstacy of love had abated somewhat. But at the time it was nothing but goodwill and affection.

The formal surrender took place on 12th September 1945 at the Municipal Building. The sky was slightly overcast, as it had been in the morning of 15th February 1942, if our memories serve us right.

The Supreme Commander, South-East Asia Command, Admiral Lord Louis Mountbatten, came from Government House by way of Stamford Road. As he passed, there were scenes of abandoned joy in the crowds lining the roads.

The Japanese delegates alighted from their cars at High Street and marched to the Municipal Building, flanked by British Military Police. As they passed, the crowds shouted *"Bakaro!"* The *"bakaros"* of thousands of throats expressed the pent-up hatred of the Nip, a hatred generated by the excesses of the Nip at his coming and deepened during the three and a half years of his occupation.

Bakaro is a word often in the mouths of the irate Nips of our acquaintance, generally going with a buffet or a kick, or both. Now, at long last, we could safely apply it to the Nip — to Nip generals! We were in luck. "I thank thee, Jew, for teaching me that word."

The commotion grew less as the Nip generals approached the granite steps of the Municipal Building, for the personages accommodated there and near there had a more highly developed sense of propriety and a greater regard for personal dignity.

The little procession turned sharply to the left and ascended the steps, disappearing into the precincts of the building. What happened there was hidden from vulgar gaze and vulgar knowledge. We waited patiently for the re-appearance of our butts.

We saw the cars of the Nip generals brought up to within fifty yards of the steps. We knew the purpose, felt disappointed, but could not help approving of the generous instinct that had prompted the gesture. It was done to save the vanquished from the contumely of the canaille massed at the periphery.

The clamour and the shouting started again the moment the Nip generals appeared. It did not continue very long, however, for the generals boarded their cars and were driven away escorted by British Military Police. As they passed, there was renewed shouting of *"Bakaro!"* Baulked of our revenge, we had perforce to reserve our lungs for a better use. As Lord Louis Mountbatten came down the steps, as he went into his car, and as he drove past, we cheered him until we were hoarse. Lord Louis stood up in his open car, saluting in acknowledgement.

Postscript

Immediately after the Japanese Occupation, the late Cheng Hui Ming suggested that we put our heads together and get out an account of what had happened during the three and a half years' nightmare that had passed. I told him that as I had kept myself in my little corner, I knew very little. But he said that, as Assistant to the Secretary for Chinese Affairs, he had access to information and records not available to the general public. He would make these available to me. The actual writing was to be my responsibility. Hui Ming died 15 years ago. Without him, there would not have been straw for brick-making, and without his slave-driving, there would have been no pyramid, however modest. The resulting book, *This Singapore*, was privately printed and distributed in 1947. The present book is largely based on that book.

Thanks are due to the Editor, *Singapore Law Journal*, for permission to draw on the late Tan Thoon Lip's *Kempeitai Kindness;* to Mrs. Lim Bo Seng for allowing me to see her husband's letters and diary; to Mr. Cheng Kuan Yew for his contribution, *On Changi Beach;* and to Mrs. Lily Keasberry for typing the manuscript twice.

To Grace Hie Ding